PHILOSOPHY OF WORLD REVOLUTION

Philosophie der Weltrevolution, Beitrag zu einer Anthologie der Revolutionstheorien, by Franz Marek was first published by Europa Verlag, Vienna, in 1966. The author has made some revisions for the English edition. The English translation is by Daphne Simon, who also compiled the Index.

PRINTED IN HUNGARY

PHILOSOPHY
OF WORLD REVOLUTION

A Contribution to an Anthology of
Theories of Revolution

FRANZ MAREK

1969
LAWRENCE & WISHART
LONDON

*Marxism is a philosophy
which is also politics,
and politics
which is also a philosophy.*

Antonio Gramsci

TRANSLATOR'S PREFACE

Franz Marek's *Philosophy of World Revolution* will, I believe, prove stimulating and useful to two groups of readers.

First, it obliges those of us who have accepted the Marxist interpretation of history and social development as a convincing one to pause and think afresh about many of the propositions which we may have come to take for granted. It is a thoroughly honest book which re-examines basic ideas like "laws of social development" and "the inevitability of socialism" and faces up to the difficulties inherent in them and the force of our opponents' criticisms. When Marek asks: If Marx's ideas are right why were there not socialist revolutions in the advanced capitalist countries long ago? why do these revolutions still look remote? he puts the question which must often be in the hearts if not the minds of all socialists in the West.

His whole method of answering is to show how Marxist ideas have undergone constant modification in face of new facts, and in the case of Marx's and Lenin's writings in particular he traces the changes in their ideas in detail, with ample illustration by quotation from their works.

Consequently his book constitutes, secondly, a very clear and valuable introduction to Marxism for the reader who would like to understand the basic concepts of the most influential ideology of our time but is, perhaps, at a loss to know where to begin. For all students of political theory it is a masterly survey, and the quotations from the sources, put in their historical contexts, are an invaluable guide to those wishing to consult the classical writers themselves.

Because of its usefulness as an introductory work on Marxism I have added some dates and a number of footnotes, chiefly on figures in the history of the European labour movement in this century who are likely to be less familiar to the English than to the Austrian reader.

Quotations from French and Italian authors have wherever possible been checked against the originals; for quotations from the Russian (and Chinese) I have relied on existing English translations.

I have given references to English translations of works referred to wherever possible. For quotations from Lenin, besides the title and date of the work, I have referred to the standard Collected Works by volume and page. Unfortunately there is no equivalent edition of Marx' and Engels' writings, so there I have given title (with date) and chapter or section.

DAPHNE SIMON

CONTENTS

National Anti-Imperialist Revolution and a Socialist Orientation
An Anti-colonial Manifesto
In Praise of Backwardness?

FOREWORD

The modern working-class movement originated and spread with the conviction that just as capitalism had superseded feudalism so socialism would inevitably supersede capitalism. Is this idea still right?

One third of mankind now lives in countries where the capitalist ownership of the means of production has either been abolished or is marked down for abolition. In the capitalist countries it has become thoroughly respectable to entertain notions — such as planning and all that — which have a sort of whiff of socialism about them. And in many of the underdeveloped countries, even in those which have no industry worth mentioning, people talk about "building socialism". Does all this prove that one may legitimately speak of the inevitability of socialist revolution? To put it more generally, is it right to think of revolutions, which have to be made by human beings, as exemplifying inexorable laws?

The title of this book (planned as the first part of a larger work) is only an approximation. The term socialist revolution is used in its basic sense and equated with the transfer of the means of production to social ownership. To revolutionary socialists the socialist revolution has always meant more than that — and since the first socialist revolution, a great deal more. This book, however, scarcely touches on that; nor does it deal at any length with the arguments about different roads to socialism and the various ways of approaching a socialist revolution. I have confined myself to the central philosophical problem of the Marxist view of history, the theory of the inevitability of the socialist revolution; to the ideas developed by Marx and Engels; to the development which their ideas have undergone; and to the deductions suggested by the development of society in our own day. That is to say, I have confronted Marxist theory and Marxist theoreticians with reality. The book is a Marxist inventory or stocktaking, and also in some ways a Marxist gleaning: it contains a lot of quotations — not proofs of anything, but documentary evidence — and these will, I hope, ensure that the work has at any rate some value as a little anthology of Marxist revolutionary theory.

I

VIEWING THE WORLD AS A CHANGING WORLD[1]

Our starting-point is this: just as in nature there are interconnections and chains of causes which men come to know about and which they can, thanks to their knowledge, utilise, apply and set in motion, so similarly in the development of society there are tendencies or large interconnections which can be referred to as laws, which we can trace out, apply in practice and set in motion. Human history is not a meaningless and accidental sequence of events; there are laws of social development which can be discovered and taken into account and whose realisation can even be speeded up on the basis of that knowledge. That is the meaning of Engels' dictum that it has become possible to study and pursue politics as a science.

The germ of this scientific way of thinking about the world lay in the thesis which (after Bacon) was formulated most clearly by Descartes in his *Discourse on Method* (1637). He expresses it thus:

"It is possible to arrive at branches of knowledge which are extremely useful to life. In place of the speculative philosophy taught in the Schools we can discover one of a practical kind, enabling us to understand the power and the workings of fire, water, air, the stars, the heavens and all the other bodies round about us as clearly as we do the different crafts of our artizans. And then in like manner we can turn this knowledge to account in whatever way may prove serviceable; and thus we may become the masters and possessors of Nature"[2].

Marxism, which has extended this thesis of Bacon's and Descartes' — that we can know nature and use this knowledge to master and change nature — to include the history of man and the development of society, has constantly found itself up against the objection: How can it be admissible to transfer a standpoint appropriate only to the natural sciences to the

---

[1] *Weltanschauung der Weltveränderung*: literally "world outlook of world change" *Weltanschauung* also has the meaning of "philosophy of life"; and *Weltveränderung* of "transforming the world"; thus see opening sentence of final chapter. (Trs.)

[2] Penguin edition (1960), p. 84.

study of society, which deals with men, with active individuals endowed with consciousness and will? Surely it is rather presumptuous to speak of laws of social development when the development of society depends on the freely willed decisions of men — a development which Marxists especially, in so far as they engage in politics, seek to influence?

Here we find ourselves up against the chief philosophical problem of that conception of history to which Marx gave his name. This does not date only from Marx, who in his principal work *Capital* quotes the words of Giovanni Battista Vico: Human history differs from natural history in that we have made the one but not made the other.[3] Strictly speaking it begins with the grand attempt made by Spinoza in his *Ethics*[4] to apply Descartes' outlook to human social intercourse and to bring human strivings and decisions into harmony with known laws, and to define "rational actions" — actions, that is, which take account of what is recognized to be necessary. As we read the *Ethics* there flickers before our eyes the Hegelian beacon, that freedom means insight into necessity.

Kant

Spinoza's limitations were the limitations of the science of his period which had not yet worked out the idea of immanent development either in nature or in society. This leap forward was made by German classical philosophy, above all by Immanuel Kant. He not only propounded an ingenious hypothesis to explain the origin and development of the solar system, but left behind fundamental ideas about the relationship between individual wills and the general development of society in conformity with certain natural laws. In his essay *Ideas for a Universal History based on the Principle of World Citizenship* (1784) we read:

"Whatever concept one may have from a metaphysical point of view regarding freedom of will, the manifestations of this in human actions are, like all other human events, determined in accordance with uni-

---

[3] Vol I, chapter 15, section 1. Vico: born in Naples, 1668, son of a poor bookseller. Became a Professor of Rhetoric at Naples University and published in 1725 *Principi d'una scienza nuova* (Principles of a new science) in which he attempted to work out a systematic philosophy of history and general laws of historical evolution based on a comparative study of civilisations, more especially their languages and laws. (Trs.)

[4] Finished c. 1665 but not published until 1677, just after his death. (Trs.)

versal natural laws. History which busies herself with recounting these manifestations, however deep their ultimate causes may lie hidden, nevertheless allows us to hope that by contemplating the interplay of free human wills on a large scale she may be able to discover within them a regular progress. And then what looks, taking particular individuals, to be confused and haphazard may — when considering the whole species — be recognisable as the slow but steadily advancing development of their original endowments."[5]

Kant underlines this idea that the accidental and arbitrary element in the decisions of individuals does not exclude the operation of laws where large numbers are involved by reference to modern statistics on births, marriages and deaths: the individual case may be fortuitous, but a lot of cases result in general interconnections and verifiable tendencies.

"Individual men (and even whole peoples) little think while they are pursuing their own purposes — each in his own way and often in direct opposition to one another — that they are advancing unconsciously under the guidance of a purpose of nature which is unknown to them and working to further her ends" (ibid).

Here there is proclaimed, albeit in the language and concepts of Kant's idealist view of the world, Frederick Engels' picture of certain natural social laws resulting from many conflicting purposes and asserting themselves through an endless succession of accidents — and, as history has developed hitherto, in a way not apparent to man's consciousness.

The recognition of this law (and here Kant anticipates Hegel) makes it possible for men to operate consciously upon developments which they have understood:

"Through the rational arrangement of our affairs we could hasten the coming of this joyous time for our successors" (ibid).

The "joyous time" which Kant hoped to hasten along corresponded to the concepts and ideals of the rising bourgeoisie. But the philosopher opposed the notion that the conviction that there are laws of development in society allows only of fatalistic conclusions. As the young Marx was to write later in a letter to Ruge, one can make even ossified social relations dance if one plays them their own dialectical tune.

[5] Translated by W. Hastie in *Eternal Peace and Other International Essays*, Boston, 1914.

Between Kant and Marx, of course, there lies the mighty mountain range of Hegel's thought. For Hegel, the most important implication of the conviction that history develops in accordance with certain laws was that it gave the study of history the dignity of a science. Human deeds and sufferings (he explained) are just what is uppermost; therefore the inquiring mind must penetrate beneath the surface so as to discover the law governing the multiplicity of appearances and grasp the general development underlying the weaknesses and passions of individual men. In so far as the strivings of human wills are concerned with trivialities they have no interest; the will that does not correspond to the broad law-governed process of development is of no effect. The laurels of the naked will are barren leaves which have never blossomed. Only that will is great and worth willing which is based on the recognition of necessity and on insight into the broad pattern of development.

In Hegel, too, is to be found the Kantian idea that men unconsciously promote the development of society in accordance with certain laws. In world events men's deeds bring to pass something other than they immediately aim at and reach for; they proceed from self-interest but something more remote comes about which had no place in their consciousness, their purpose or their knowledge:

> "But in the process of the World's History itself — as still incomplete — the abstract final aim of history is not yet made the distinct object of desire and interest. While these limited sentiments are still unconscious of the purpose they are fulfilling, the universal principle is implicit in them, and is realizing itself through them . . .
>
> "This may be called the cunning of reason — that it sets the passions to work for itself, while that which develops its existence through such impulsion pays the penalty and suffers loss. For it is phenomenal being that is so treated, and of this, part is of no value, part is positive and real. The particular is for the most part of trifling value compared with the general: individuals are sacrificed and abandoned. The idea pays the penalty of determinate existence and of corruptibility, not from itself, but from the passions of individuals."[6]

[6] G. W. F. Hegel. *The Philosophy of History*, trans. J. Sibtree (New York) pp. 25—26, 33.

14

This grand integration of the individual will with a general development conforming to certain laws produced an anguished protest from Kierkegaard.[7] Every system, he wrote — he shrieked — cuts right through living men and allows of corpses only. Man — suffering, hoping, fearing death — cannot be comprehended in a system of historical philosophy. Idiosyncrasy and individuality cannot be understood as part of a scientifically knowable pattern. In reality the Universal consists simply of the individual, with his responsibility and his power to make decisions, and his despair.

This revolt against the idea of general laws of development may at times of rapid change and social crisis become — as Marx once wrote — a weapon of those forces which sigh over the past, despair of the present and fear the future. But recognition of the historical effectiveness of an ideology is still no answer to the philosophical problems which it raises. Kierkegaard's outcry confronts us with the chief problem of every philosophy of evolution, of every philosophy of revolution.

Marx's Law of Motion

Marx and Engels took over from Hegel the conviction that history is not a collection of imaginary actions of imaginary men, nor a mass of bare facts, nor a meaningless succession of unconnected happenings. A world outlook of changing the world, the conception of being able to have a powerful influence upon events thanks to understanding their interconnections in history — Marx and Engels founded this idea upon the law of motion of history, by which they explained the succession of the various forms of society and the rhythm of this succession.

The relations in which men live and get their livelihood, largely conditioned by the circumstance of who owns the decisive means of production, they called the relations of production (or production relations: *Produktionsverhältnisse*). The tools and instruments which men employ in their struggle with nature, and also the methods and forms of work, and the knowledge with which the perfecting of these tools is bound up, they called the forces

---

[7] Søren Kierkegaard, 1813—55. A Danish philosopher, often called the father of existentialism. A strict Calvinist, he saw sin as the great reality, and the world as a battleground for mural struggle. He distrusted the advances of science and democracy and all attempts to embody truth in a philosophical 'System'. Truth was to be apprehended subjectively, on the basis of the individual's total *existence*. Not translated at all until after 1918, his works have had their main influence since 1939 — not least owing to Sartre (see Chapter 6). (Trs.)

of production (or productive forces: *Produktivkräfte*). And what their law of motion said was that in the history of the forms of human society there is a constant tendency for the relations of production to come into harmony with the level of development of the productive forces, so that in the end property relations are bound to conform to the development of the productive forces. In the famous perface to the *Critique of Political Economy* (1859) Marx wrote:

> "In the social production of their life, men enter into definite relations that are indispensable and independent of their will, relations of production that correspond to a definite stage of development of their material productive forces . . . At a certain stage of their development the material productive forces of society come into conflict with the existing relations of production or — what is but a legal expression for the same thing — with the property relations within which they have been at work hitherto. From forms of development of the productive forces these relations turn into their fetters. Then begins an epoch of social revolution."

Leaving aside the complicated problem of mixed and transitional forms of society and neglecting too, for the sake of simplicity, the peculiarities of the ancient Asiatic modes of production, which Marx refers to, we can recognise primitive communism, slavery, feudalism, capitalism and socialism as being the principal forms of society. And, a hundred years after the formulation of the law of motion, we have no more plausible explanation for these forms being superseded in the way they have been, or for the fact that different forms of society are succeeding one another at an ever swifter pace thanks to the accelerating rate of development of the productive forces.

If Marx and Engels occasionally compared the operation of the law of motion of society to a "process of natural history" and referred to it as the "natural law" of social development, they also stressed often enough that comparing historical tendencies with natural laws requires the utmost caution. In human history nothing happens without human beings, but — as Kant had already explained — over and beyond individual endeavours and actions general connections and tendencies assert themselves which can be recognised, manipulated and furthered. Men are the bearers of a reality which changes itself and also the originators of a change which they themselves bring to pass; they are both the authors of and the actors in the historical drama. Once they have hit upon the track of the law of motion they can take it into account consciously and scientifically. They can work in harmony with it and, as it says in the preface to the first volume of *Capital* (1867), so shorten and lessen the birth-pangs of the new society.

So the world outlook which stands at the cradle of modern thought found its crowning achievement in the philosophy of revolution. The cunning of reason arranged things so that exactly three hundred years after the Holy Office had damned the *Discours de la Méthode* for presumption the papal encyclical *Pacem in Terris* echoed Descartes' memorable formulas and extolled the intelligence and power of Man armed with knowledge.

THE LAW OF MOTION AND THE PHILOSOPHY OF MOTION

From the law of motion of history Marx and Engels deduced the thesis of the inevitability of the socialist revolution, and this lent wings to the development of the modern working-class movement. "Property relations, the relations of production, are burst asunder if they become fetters upon the growth of the productive forces. Just as capitalism followed feudalism, so socialism is bound to follow capitalism." This complicated historical philosophical argument became the creed of millions of workers who, as Engels wrote in *Ludwig Feuerbach*, had an interest in recognising the law of development of history and were responsive to it.

In various ways, with varying emphases and minor corrections, what Marx and Engels stressed again and again was that with the growth of the productive forces their socialised character grows too, and this expresses itself in the formation of large enterprises, in the increasing co-operation brought about by advances in technology and the interweaving of individual production processes, and in the decisive importance of industrial production for society. But the growth of the productive forces is more and more hampered by capitalist property relations and their social character stands in growing contrast to the private ownership of the means of production and the private appropriation of the resultant products. Crises and pauperism are the eloquent witnesses to a development which (as Marx wrote in 1853) runs its course with the same necessity as the geological revolutions which have created the surface of the earth.[1]

Already in 1848 the *Communist Manifesto* hammers home the powerful comparison:

"At a certain stage in the development of these means of production and of exchange, the conditions under which feudal society produced and exchanged, the feudal organisation of agriculture and manufacturing industry, in one word, the feudal relations of property, became no longer compatible with the already developed productive forces; they hindered production instead of promoting it; they became so

[1] In his article for the *New York Daily Tribune* of 8th August 1853 entitled "The Future Results of British Rule in India".

many fetters. They had to be burst asunder; they were burst asunder.

Into their place stepped free competition, accompanied by a social and political constitution adapted to it, and by the economical and political sway of the bourgeoisie.

A similar movement is going on before our very eyes. Modern bourgeois society with its relations of production, of exchange and of property, a society that has conjured up such gigantic means of production and exchange, is like the sorcerer who is no longer able to control the powers of the nether world whom he has called up by his spells. For many a decade past the history of industry and commerce is but the history of the revolt of the modern productive forces against modern conditions of production, against the property relations that are the conditions for the existence of the bourgeoisie and its rule."[2]

The *Manifesto* points to the economic crises which "put the existence of the entire bourgeois society on its trial, each time more threateningly". These "epidemics of overproduction" prove that the capitalist relations of production have become too narrow to contain the wealth they have created. The destruction of productive forces during crises, the conquest of new markets, and the thorough exploitation of the old markets, therefore, only pave the way "for more extensive and more destructive crises" and diminish the possibility of preventing them. Similiarly the increasing pauperism confirms that capitalist property relations are becoming inconsistent with the growth of the productive forces. The bourgeoisie become incapable of ensuring an existence to their slaves within their slavery. Society can no longer live under the bourgeoisie, that is to say, their life is no longer compatible with that of society.

The most comprehensive and popular presentation of the law of motion of economics and of the thesis of the inevitability of the socialist revolution is to be found next in those chapters of *Anti-Dühring* which Engels put together under the title *Socialism: Utopian and Scientific* — after the *Manifesto* undoubtedly the most widely circulated piece of polemical writing in the modern working-class movement at the turn of the century. Nearly thirty years after the *Manifesto* it develops the basic ideas of the Marxist philosophy of history, with greater subtlety, in part more cautiously, in part more clearly and concretely.

[2] From the first section, entitled "Bourgeois and Proletarians".

The incompatibility between social production and capitalist appropriation becomes ever more glaring. It exhibits itself in the contrast between the organisation of production in the individual factory and the anarchy of production in society as a whole and leads to that "defective circulation" "which moves in the form of a spiral and must meet its end, like the motion of the planets, by collision with the centre".[3] On the one hand (and here Engels repeats the general law of capitalist accumulation worked out by Marx in *Capital*) the improvement of machines leads to the displacement of workers and the creation of an industrial reserve army of disposible wage-earners who are separated into a layer of paupers as inevitably as electrolysis decomposes water into hydrogen and oxygen. On the other hand, the expansion of the market cannot keep pace with the expansion of production, and this leads inevitably to periodic crises. In these crises the contradiction between social production and private appropriation results in a violent explosion. True, these crises are not spoken of here (as they are in the *Manifesto*) as getting constantly more acute and widespread — a formula which Marx still echoed in the preface to the second edition of the first volume of *Capital*.[4] But the conclusion is identical: "The mode of production rebels against the mode of exchange."[5]

Simultaneously, the contradiction between the private appropriation of the product (the mode of exchange) and the social character of the productive forces gets sharper. In the competition of the capitalists with each other the small capitalists are destroyed by the big ones and there follows a centralisation of capital both as regards the ownership of the means of production and the appropriation of the products; and on the other hand the forces of production compel practical recognition of their social nature, even within the framework of capitalist property relations. The formation of joint-stock companies and monopolistic mergers and, above all, the transference of important sections of production and exchange to state ownership demonstrates the force of the development; the un-

[3] Engels: *Socialism, Utopian and Scientific*, section iii (first published in English in 1892).

[4] (Final paragraph). Marx refers to "contradictions inherent in the movement of capitalist society ... whose crowning point is the universal crisis", points out that "that crisis is once again approaching, although as yet but in its preliminary stage" and calls attention to its "universality" and "intensity". This preface was written in January, 1873, the year which saw the beginning of "the great depression" which lasted, with only short breaks, until 1896. (Trs.)

[5] Engels, *op. cit.*, section iii.

planned production of capitalist society capitulates (at first still to the benefit and advantage of the capitalists) to the planned production of the incipient socialist society. As regards social production, as regards production for society, the bourgeoisie can now be dispensed with; the capitalist forfeits his function to society and to history; state ownership of the productive forces is not, as yet, the solution of the great conflict, but it is the mechanism for solving it.

"This solution can only consist in the practical recognition of the social nature of the modern forces of production, and therefore in the harmonising of the modes of production, appropriation and exchange with the social character of the means of production. And this can only come about by society openly and directly taking possession of the productive forces which have outgrown all control except that of society itself. The social character of the means of production and of the products today reacts against the producers, periodically disrupts all production and exchange, and acts only like a law of nature working blindly, forcibly, destructively. But with the taking over by society of the productive forces, the social character of the means of production and of the products will be utilised by the producers with a perfect understanding of its nature, and instead of being a source of disturbance and periodical collapse will become the most powerful lever of production itself."[6]

Law of Development — Law of Revolution

Insight into the way social development conforms to certain laws, and then intervention in developments on the basis of that insight: the law of motion of history contains the key to the socialist revolution. Social development happens of necessity, but necessity is realised through social forces. The sharpness of the conflict between the character of the productive forces and their development, on the one side, and capitalist property relations, on the other, was represented by Marx and Engels as an objective process which was often compared with the processes of natural history. Marx accepted the view of a Russian writer who compared the way historical development conforms to certain laws with the processes of biology, and who wrote of Marx that: "From the necessity of the existing

[6] Ibid.

order of things he proves at the same time the necessity of another order into which the first will inevitably be transformed quite regardless of whether men believe in it or not, and whether they are conscious of it or not. Marx regards the movement of society as a process of natural history governed by laws which are not merely independent of the wills and consciousness and designs of men but which rather, on the contrary, determine their wills, consciousness and designs."[7] And in the foreword to the first English edition of his book *The Condition of the Working Class in England in 1844* (1892) Engels reprints an article of his published in 1885 in which, speaking of the sharpening of the decisive contradiction of capitalist production, he said:

"Its lifeblood is the necessity of continuous expansion and this continuous expansion now becomes impossible. Capitalist production runs into a blind alley."

But already in their youthful writings Marx and Engels were stressing that the inevitability of the socialist revolution inevitably involves the recognition of its inevitability. In *The Holy Family* (1845) they remark that it is the task of the proletariat, to which its historical situation obviously and irrevocably destines it, to take action to set historical development free, and to execute sentence upon capitalist private property which, by its creation of the proletariat, has brought the sentence upon itself. The advance of capitalist production, declares the *Manifesto*, "replaces the isolation of the labourers, due to competition, by their revolutionary combination, due to association. The development of modern industry, therefore, cuts from under the feet of the bourgeoisie the very foundation on which it produces and appropriates products. What the bourgeoisie therefore produces, above all, are its own gravediggers. Its fall and the victory of the proletariat are equally inevitable."[8]

In his *Socialism, Utopian and Scientific* Engels expressly states that the contradiction between social production and capitalist appropriation is revealed in the antagonism of proletariat and bourgeoisie and that it is the task of the proletariat to secure due recognition of the social character of production (made manifest in the growing importance of state ownership in the means of production) by the seizure of state power. The

[7] From a Russian review of *Capital*, quoted by Marx in his preface to its second German edition.

[8] Final paragraph of the first section, "Bourgeois and Proletarians".

nature and character of the productive forces, which have hitherto asserted themselves in an elemental way without the aid of men and even in opposition to them can, when they are recognised and respected for what they are, be so planned and regulated as to make production the servant of society.

Thus according to Marx and Engels the force of the pace of economic development also inevitably involves action and defiance and struggle on the part of the class which is battling its way through to the socialist revolution. As Engels puts it in one of his articles on *Capital*, the development of capitalist production creates the very force which is compelled to take it over. And in one of the most eloquent passages of *Capital* itself we read:

> "Along with the constantly diminishing number of the magnates of capital, who usurp and monopolise all advantages of this process of transformation, grows the mass of misery, oppression, slavery, degradation, exploitation; but with this too grows the revolt of the working class, a class always increasing in numbers, and disciplined, united, organised by the very mechanism of the process of capitalist production itself. The monopoly of capital becomes a fetter on the mode of production, which has sprung up and flourished along with and under it. Centralisation of the means of production and socialisation of labour at last reach a point where they become incompatible with their capitalist integument. This integument is burst asunder. The knell of capitalist private property sounds. The expropriators are expropriated."[9]

These lines, dealing with the compelling power of an irresistible process, also voice the conviction that it is the revolt of organised labour and the growing organisation of the expropriated which bring this process to realisation. And it is put in a similar way in Marx's *The Civil War in France* (1871):

> "The working class did not expect miracles from the Commune. They have no ready-made utopias to introduce *par décret du peuple*. They know that in order to work out their own emancipation, and along with it that higher form to which present society is irresistibly tending through its own economic development, they will have to

[9] *Capital*, Chapter 32, Historical Tendency of Capitalist Accumulation.

pass through long struggles, through a series of historical processes, in the course of which men, no less than circumstances, will be completely transformed. They have no ideals [here used in the sense of speculative concepts — F.M.] to realise, other than to set free the elements of the new society which has already developed within the womb of the collapsing bourgeois society."[10]

[10] Section iii.

3

THE THEORY BECOMES A FORCE

In the same way, Marx's pupils, heirs and popularisers also presented the law of motion of society as a philosophy of motion; they were convinced that socialism would supersede capitalism, but this conviction included the certainty that it would increasingly become the conviction of most men, above all of the workers. Consequently the suggestion that the mounting contradiction between production and property relations finds expression in "overproduction and increasing misery"[1] became more subtle and cautious as capitalism and the working-class movement developed.

The declarations in the programmes of the avowedly Marxist parties also recall the figures of speech and formulations of the classical texts. For example, in the Hainfeld programme of the Austrian Social-Democrats[2] (1888—9) it said:

> "Private ownership of the means of production . . . means, in the economic field, mounting mass poverty and growing misery for ever broader sections of the people.
>
> Thanks to technical developments and the colossal growth of the productive forces this form of ownership is not merely proving superfluous; for the overwhelming majority of the people it is actually being abolished while at the same time the essential spiritual and material preconditions are being created for a form of common ownership. The transference of the means of employment to the common ownership of the whole working people will mean not only the

[1] Engels in *Ludwig Feuerbach* (1888).

[2] "Social-Democratic Party" was the usual name assumed by socialist parties in Europe before 1914. They contained both left (Marxist) and right wings. They were usually affiliated to the "Second International" founded in 1889 to unite all parties which recognized the class struggle as the basis for their work. (The *first* "International Working Men's Association", founded in 1864, and in which Marx played a leading part, had come to an end soon after the defeat of the Paris Commune in 1871.) These parties were pledged to oppose any wars by their governments. In fact, in 1914, all but a minority in each supported the war. This divided the parties and discredited the name Social-Democrat in revolutionary eyes, and so altered its meaning. (Trs.)

liberation of the working class but also the fulfilment of an historically necessary development. This development can only be brought about by the class-conscious proletariat, organised in a political party."

Similarly the Erfurt programme of the German Social-Democrats (1891) declared that it was a "necessity of nature" that small business was bringing about its own downfall, and deduced the socialist revolution from the fact that the forces of production had outgrown the limits of bourgeois society and that economic development was leading irresistibly to the bankruptcy of the capitalist method of production.

The Bernstein Controversy

At the turn of the century the philosophical problem of the law of motion of society — both necessity and conscious decision, the inevitability of the socialist revolution and also the mobilisation of the proletariat for revolution — developed in the course of the revisionist controversy from a problem which was part of the contest between the working-class movement and their opponents into a subject of argument inside the working-class movement itself. Eduard Bernstein's[3] chief philosophical objection to the masters and their pupils was based on his separation and cleavage of the unity of the two concepts. One could only properly speak of necessity (he said) if men were automatons. Determinism in history must lead to fatalism, which leaves no room for conscious decision or moral feelings about right and wrong. Moreover, the "inevitable necessity" of economic and social processes does not correspond to the facts. A rising standard of living, trade union struggles and also adaptations made by capitalism itself (whose increasing concentration Bernstein contested) contradict the Marxist "theory of collapse" — the expression originates with Bernstein — a theory which (he said) had anyway never been compatible with Marx' and Engels' own scientific research.

Karl Kautsky's answer — more especially his *Bernstein und das social-demokratische Programm* (Bernstein and the Programme of the Social

---

[3] Eduard Bernstein 1847—1932, German Social-Democrat, journalist and theoretician, for some years member of the Reichstag, became the chief champion of 'revisionism' and 'reformism' i.e. of *revising* Marx's theories so as to demonstrate that a socialist revolution was unnecessary, that the workers could get all they wanted by *reforms* within capitalism. His book *Voraussetzungen des Sozialismus* (Pre-requisites of Socialism) 1898 became the gospel of the right wing of the labour movement on the continent for a generation. (Trs.)

Democrats, 1899) — was drawn in essentials from the classical texts which document the inseparable dialectical unity of law and action.[4] In that way Kautsky avoided laying down that an economic crisis was the prelude to the seizure of power by the proletariat — and actually, only a year later, one of those very economic crises occurred which Bernstein had pointed to as having been overcome. Also Kautsky did not deduce increasing misery — which quite rightly, following Marx, he did not equate with a fall in real wages — from the general law of capitalist accumulation and the tendency towards an increase in pauperism; that was to a certain extent a modification of the idea which Marx and Engels had often used to demonstrate the contradiction between the growth of the productive forces and bourgeois property relations.

In opposition to what he had called the "theory of collapse" Bernstein coined the slogan: "Back to Kant". What he chiefly had in mind, however, was the philosopher's moral law, not his reflections on the philosophy of history — to which indeed Bernstein might have made exactly the same objection as he did to Marxist historical philosophy. The neo-Kantian philosopher Max Adler, for example, who expressly emphasized that the contradiction between the forces of production and the relations of production would be resolved through class struggle and the victory of the working class, and that this would also be "a victory for morality, justice and reason", repeated at the same time that this victory would grow — in Kant's and Marx's sense — "out of social conditions with a force that would finally be irresistible"; and he spoke of a "wonderful mechanism".[5]

Rosa Luxemburg

In the course of the controversy with revisionism Rosa Luxemburg developed a genuine theory of collapse; it was a deliberate correction of the Marxist model of accumulation. This outstanding Marxist emphasised the twofold character of social development (the working of objective laws alongside social activity, the sharpening of social contradictions beside the maturing of the proletariat) but, persisting in the idea that an

[4] Karl Kautsky 1854—1938. Born in Prague, later settled in Germany. Editor of *Neue Zeit* from 1883 to 1917. One of the leading Marxist theoreticians in the Second International. He veered increasingly to the right and became a strong opponent of the Russian revolution. (Trs.)

[5] *Marxistische Probleme* (Problems of Marxism), Stuttgart, 1913 p. 44.

economic crisis would probably be the starting point for the proletariat seizing power, she built up the idea of development conforming with certain objective laws into a new theory of accumulation. The existence of the capitalist system depends on its being able to realise the surplus value derived from unpaid labour; this, Rosa Luxemburg now tried to show, could only be achieved in a non-capitalist environment, either in the agricultural economy of the home country or in agrarian colonies.

"But through this process capitalism prepares its downfall, in two respects. On the one hand by expanding at the expense of the non-capitalist forms of production it is heading for the moment when the whole of mankind will indeed consist solely of capitalists and wage earners and then any further expansion, and therefore accumulation, will be impossible. At the same time, in proportion as this tendency asserts itself, class struggles will sharpen, and the international economic and political anarchy will be such that, long before we have reached the logical end of economic development and the absolute undivided sovereignty of capitalist production in the world, it will have brought about the rebellion of the international proletariat against the existence of capitalist rule."[6]

Thus Rosa Luxemburg attributed the anarchy of the capitalist system, together with the sharpened contradiction between the social character of production and the private appropriation of the product, above all to the industrialisation of the agricultural sector as a result of capitalist accumulation. Consequently the opening up of new markets under imperialism is both a means of prolonging the existence of capitalism, and also the surest means and shortest way, objectively, of bringing its existence to an end. Once the domination of the world by capitalist production is reached, any further accumulation becomes impossible: "Capitalism gets into a blind alley . . . it reaches its objective limits." The historical necessity of the socialist revolution which the proletariat carries through derives from this "blind alley".

[6] Die Akkumulation des Kapitals (The Accumulation of Capital), Berlin, 1923, pp. 396—7 (Translated by Agnes Schwarzchild, with an introduction by Joan Robinson. 1951) Rosa Luxemburg 1870—1919: by birth a Pole, she became one of the greatest leaders of the German Social-Democratic Party. Along with Karl Liebknecht she opposed the war in 1914 and formed the Spartacus League to campaign for proletarian internationalism. A few months after helping to found the German Communist Party they were assassinated by army officers. (Trs.)

With Rosa Luxemburg the 'natural historical' side of the law of motion of society and of the socialist revolution takes an original and extreme form. She drew this lopsided picture (understandably, it seems to me) and made it the leading concept of a mass movement which had to put the revolutionary character of the new theory in the forefront and which drew strength and confidence from a necessary distortion which, strictly speaking, already followed from the classical texts, especially from Engels.

The Russian Marxists

The line of inheritance of Marxism that led to the first revolution to be headed by Marxists is an interesting one. Amongst the Russian Marxists Plekhanov's popularisation and interpretation of Marxism made a lasting impression.[7] It corresponded in essentials with the train of ideas in the classics, but with a heavy emphasis on "natural historical processes". In his book *The Role of the Individual in History* Plekhanov wrote of capitalism proceeding "along the path of its own development to its own negation" so that Marxists are "the tools of necessity". Determinism does not mean the same as fatalism, but even fatalism — the denial of any free will — would not mean the renunciation of revolutionary activity, as the critics of Marxism always maintain. Fatalistic views have not hindered Mohammedans and Calvinists from displaying intense activity; and individuals who delude themselves that they are chosen by providence are capable of developing immense activity filled with the conviction that they must needs act so because they cannot do otherwise. The idea of necessary development is an inspiration and increases the driving force of action; taking part in an inevitable development means "that I regard my deeds as one link in a chain of circumstances which in its entirety necessarily guarantees the victory of the movement".[8]

Plekhanov's emphasis on the 'natural historical' is given its starkest expression when he comes to estimate the role of the individual in history.

[7] G. V. Plekhanov 1856—1918. The leading Russian Marxist before Lenin. Founded the first group of Russian Marxists in 1883 to oppose the Narodniks (See Chapter 6, note 1) and helped to found the Russian Social-Democratic Party. He belonged to its Menshevik ('minority') or right wing, and did not join the Bolshevik ('majority') or left wing in opposing the 1914 war. (Trs.)

[8] G. V. Plekhanov, *Fundamental Problems of Marxism*, section xvi (first published 1908).

Here he takes the simplification already made by Engels (if Napoleon had never lived some other general would have filled his place) and intensifies and vulgarises it still further.[9]

Lenin, in his first theoretical work *Who the Friends of the People Are* (1894) set himself to counter the traditional objection of a critic of Marxism, that the idea of an economic law of motion in history and a belief in the irresistible approach of socialism treats men as "marionettes, manipulated from a mysterious underground by the immanent laws of historical necessity". The law of motion of society, Lenin answered, is the basis of the conviction about the inevitability of socialism. The forms of appropriation of the product have to give way and adapt themselves to the development of the productive forces, but a proper understanding of this development elicits the right answer to the question of when there is the best guarantee that our activity will be crowned with success. "The idea of determinism, which postulates that human acts are necessitated and rejects the absurd tale about free-will, in no way destroys either man's reason or his conscience."[10]

Here the problem is stated rather than discussed. It is one of the legends of social-democratic theoreticians that Lenin abandoned Marx's thesis that social development follows certain laws and replaced it with a subjective voluntarism. Actually Lenin emphasised the basic idea of historical materialism that "out of one form of social life, as the result of the growth of the productive forces, another higher form develops;"[11] and he reiterated that Marx had demonstrated the inevitability of the transformation of capitalist society into a socialist one, and that he had derived this from the economic law of motion of modern society.[12] It seems to me that Lenin was much more consistent and logical than other Marxists in following up Marx and Engels' suggestion that the socialisation of labour and production represents the material basis for the inevitable victory of socialism. And he was clearer than the other Marxists in finding formulations and working out ideas which overcame Plekhanov's one-sidedness and gave the dialectical unity of the law of motion of society its true value.

[9] G. V. Plekhanov, *The Role of the Individual in History*, section vii (first published 1898).
[10] Lenin, Collected Works, Vol. 1 p. 159.
[11] Lenin, *The Three Sources and Three Component Parts of Marxism* (1913). Collected Works Vol. 19 p. 25.
[12] Lenin, *Karl Marx* (1914). Collected Works Vol. 21 p. 71.

Theory becomes a force if it grips the masses, the young Marx had written;[13] and the theory of the historical law of motion did become a force, because it gripped the working masses in many countries. But for that very reason it acquired some of the features of folklore: 'the iron laws of history' became a consolation and a spur; 'the world is ours, despite all' a comfort and a reassurance. The more it was popularised the more it was vulgarised. By way of example take Stalin's first great theoretical work, *Anarchism and Socialism* (1906) written in the popular style then current:

> "Modern industrial crises, which are tolling capitalist ownership to its grave and which decidedly pose the question: either capitalism or socialism, reveal intuitively ... the inevitability of socialism ... Since now the private character of ownership does not correspond to the social character of production, since modern collective work must lead inevitably to collective ownership, it is self-evident that the socialist order must follow capitalism with the same inevitability *as day follows night.*"[14]

The conviction of an inevitable iron law of development towards socialism, of its following capitalism as day follows night, allows of two conclusions: the pleasant feeling of objective development reaching its final end without any particular exertions, and also — as Plekhanov had already indicated — heightened activity so as to bring the invincible to fulfilment. It was to refuting the first sort of conclusion, and showing how it amounted to opportunist ideas labelling themselves as Marxist in the working-class movement, that Lenin addressed himself, above all in *What is to be Done?* (1902).[15] In social-democratic literature this work has come to be valued as, at best, a guide to the formation of an illegal organisation of professional revolutionaries, and as the expression of Lenin's overestimate of the possibilities of such an organisation — very understandable, too, in the difficult conditions of Tsarist Russia — as a book whose interest lies simply in the place it occupies in the history of the Russian working-class movement and the Bolsheviks. However, we value it as the most important book published after the death of Marx and Engels on the fundamental problem of the Marxist philosophy of history.

---

[13] In his *Contribution to the Critique of Hegel's Philosophy of Law* (1844).
[14] Stalin's italics.
[15] Collected Works Vol. 5 pp. 347—528.

Appealing to Marxism for support, the Russian version of opportunism made a respect for objective development an excuse for rejecting any bold approach and any revolutionary activity, and demanded adaptation to the spontaneous process of development. As against this, Lenin developed from the Marxist view of history "demands for mass consciousness in theoretical as well as in political and organisational work;" and that (he said) means using the flashes of light which are released in the minds of working men by the lessons drawn from particular experiences and developments to raise consciousness and understanding to a higher level. Because — as Engels wrote and Lenin constantly stressed — Marxism is not a dogma, it is a guide to action, a source of initiative and energy; it opens up the widest possible perspectives for revolutionaries.

In their presentation of the law of motion of society the popularisers and vulgarisers of Marxism had stressed the 'natural historical' side more and more. *What is to be Done?* was called forth by the exigencies of politics but it was significant philosophically too because it was a timely warning against the growing distortion and vulgarisation of Marxist philosophy which was taking all the life out of the Marxist law of motion and reducing it to a fatalistic theory of self-propulsion.

Neo-Darwinism

The warning went unheeded in the writings of those Marxists who were turning the Marxist view of history into a sort of biology, a neo-Darwinism. This applies first and foremost to Karl Kautsky, who had come into the working-class movement as a Darwinist. He applied the concepts of heredity and adaptation to environment to his view of the law of social development. "What looks like an advance in development is really adaptation to new conditions of life" so that "the history of mankind is only a special illustration of the history of all living matter; it has its own special laws but these are in accordance with the general laws governing animate Nature."[16]

Kautsky granted that men differ from animals because they can achieve an "active adaptation" and can change the environment they have in-herited by creating tools and forms of organisation. But his biological

[16] *Die materialistische Geschichtsauffassung* (The Materialist Conception of History) Berlin 1927. Vol. I p. 406.

determinism left very little play for the human will and its decisions. In particular, the concept of "productive forces" is used in a rather narrower sense than can be deduced from the various contexts in which Marx and Engels use it. With them we find that the concept includes not only tools and other aids to labour, scientific knowledge and improvements in production, but also the way in which work is organised and so, in the last resort, the men who create these things. It was only logical if Kautsky in his biological determinism narrowed down these decisive forces of production to technique, and indicated in his works on the problems of ethics that even morality was determined by the development of the productive forces, and deduced the inevitable perfecting of morals from the growth of the productive forces.

Similar modes of thought, but in an even cruder form, are to be found in Bukharin's *Historical Materialism* (1921). Society adapts itself to nature and struggles to achieve an equilibrium which is always upset again by the growth of the productive forces, so that through active adaptation a new balance has to be struggled for. Thus the productive forces, whose development is decisive for the development of society, are reduced by Bukharin, even more clearly than by Kautsky, just to techniques. Accordingly, Bukharin declared that it was the task of historical materialism to translate and transform the Hegelian dialectic "into the language of modern mechanics".[17]

These vulgar versions of the Marxist law of motion of society were often referred to as "the theory of the productive forces". They led to the contradictory conclusions mentioned above which degraded Marxism from a guide to action into a justification for inaction and into a scientific apologetic for defeats suffered and opportunities missed — an apologetic which used Marxist concepts to prove that the defeat was inevitable. The "iron law" coupled the inevitability of the final victory with the inevitability of defeats on the road to victory.

But "the theory of the productive forces" also served as a basis for the belief that everything can be achieved, that victory is indeed inevitable. Rosa Luxemburg was the personification of the possibility of reconciling

[17] *Historical Materialism: a System of Sociology* (New York, 1925). N. I. Bukharin, a Russian revolutionary and theoretician, joined the Bolsheviks in 1906 and held a number of leading positions after the Revolution both in the Russian Communist Party and in the Communist International. But he was in opposition to Stalin on a number of issues. He was arrested in 1937 and executed in 1938. (Trs.)

a "theory of collapse" with a revolutionary spirit that stormed the heavens. And the history of the Russian Marxists, too, is rich in documents illustrating this, from the first programme of the victorious Bolsheviks who designated the triumph of the October revolution "an inevitable consequence of the development of capitalism" to Stalin's proclamation that there are no fortresses which Bolsheviks cannot capture.

INTERVENTION FROM BEHIND PRISON WALLS

After a long period of popularisation and vulgarisation of the law of motion of society the time came for a philosophical reappraisal. It duly followed, but it remained virtually unknown.

Between 1929 and 1935 Antonio Gramsci — imprisoned, destined to die and struggling against ill-health and fascist surveillance — wrote down thoughts which to my mind represent the most outstanding contribution made by any Marxist to the discussion of the basic problem of the Marxist philosophy of history. They are to be found chiefly in the first volume of Gramsci's collected works: *Il materialismo storico e la filosofia di Benedetto Croce* (Historial Materialism and the Philosophy of Benedetto Croce).

Gramsci's starting-point was that the popularisation of Marxism in the modern working-class movement had made a "fasa popularesca" inevitable, and that in this phase, to have a determinist and mechanical element constituting the "ideological aroma of the philosophy of praxis" — the name Gramsci gave to Marxism in his prison writings, and not only because of the censor, either — was historically understandable in a theory which gripped the masses:

"When you have not got the initiative in the struggle, and the struggle ends in a series of defeats, then mechanical determinism becomes a formidable source of moral resistance, of solidarity and of patient, obstinate perserverance. 'For the moment I have suffered a defeat, but in the long run the force of things is working in my favour' etc. The real will is transformed into an act of faith . . . into an empirical and primitive form of impassioned finalism *(appassianato finalismo)* which serves as a substitute for the predestination, providence, etc: of the confessional religions. It must be emphasized that even in such circumstances there exists in reality a strong active will, a direct influence on the 'force of things', but in an implicit, veiled form which is ashamed of itself . . ."[1]

[1] Antonio Gramsci: *Il Materialismo Storico*, 1948. pp. 13—14.

But if the revolutionary movement develops into a leading force responsible for the activities of broad masses of people, then this mechanistic outlook becomes a real danger. Now far-reaching decisions have to be made and great responsibilities undertaken: Gramsci did not live to see the day when the danger would consist precisely in the fact that people would lay claim to infallibility for their decisions on the ground that they reflected the objective working of natural laws. Gramsci stressed that a mechanistic interpretation of the law of motion of society, understandable enough as a philosophy of the broad masses, will not do as the foundation of a dialectical philosophy. The time has come to "pronounce a funeral eulogy upon it, vindicating its usefulness for a certain period but precisely because of this urging the necessity of burying it with full honours"[2].

In the last resort the creative power of Marxism does not consist in the fact that it proves that there is no historical reality which exists independently of human beings but in its showing that this reality always exists in association with human beings who change it. What would historical objectivity be without the activity of men, who create all values? Just chaos, nothingness. It is impossible to separate activity from matter, or subject from object, without landing in a kind of religion, a senseless abstraction. Therefore the transition of socialism from science to action, and the transformation of Marxist theory into the dominant theory of a state, has world-wide significance as "the real dialectic" of Marxism and "the real criticism" of Marxist philosophy. And that is where Lenin's importance as a philosopher comes in.

In contrast to Plekhanov's interpretation, which Gramsci criticised as being a crude sort of materialism, Gramsci called historical laws "laws of tendency" and said that they should not be interpreted in the same sense as the laws of natural history or in the spirit of a speculative determinism. There are certain conformities to certain laws, there are certain tendencies, and consequently it is possible to some extent to foresee how things will develop — but not in a metaphysical, determinist sense. The vulgarisation of Marxist historical philosophy has revived the need to reiterate at a later stage Marx's first thesis on Feuerbach (1845):

"The chief defect of all materialism hitherto . . . is that the thing, reality, sensuousness is conceived only in the form of the object or of

[2] Ibid p. 19.

contemplation, but not as human sensuous activity, praxis, not sub-jectively."[3]

At this later stage the "objectivisation" of the law of motion of society, resulting from the popularisation of the Marxist philosophy of history, has indeed proved to be entirely compatible with a maximum of activity. Bukharin's book, *Historical Materialism*, is a good illustration of this. This book was subjected by Gramsci to a searching criticism, seasoned with biting irony, as being a simplification of the Marxist conception of history which, by appealing to common-sense, gave the impression that you could use a mechanical formula to stuff the whole of history into your pocket. The consequences are "spiritual laziness" and "propagandist superficiality", if no account is taken of the fact that the concrete moments of the struggle cannot be determined beforehand but that, on the contrary, they are the result of conflicting forces which are permanently in motion. The mechan-istic myth may have served some purpose in the past, but it is as useless for giving a scientific picture of the past as it is for helping with the problems confronting us in the future, because it simply blots out the criterion of choice, alternatives and decisions.

It is characteristic of this vulgarisation that it reduces the material forces of production, as Bukharin did, to tools first and foremost. Gramsci dubbed it a "baroque" attitude if people, for the sake of orthodoxy, take account only of the most material objects. What about libraries, labora-tories and mathematical formulas: are they not part of the productive forces?

Gramsci's notebooks were first published after Italy's liberation from fascism, some ten to twenty years after they had been written. The fact that they have remained almost unknown outside Italy, even in the world Communist movement, is bound up with all that side of things that is summed up in the notion of the cult of personality. Making a fetish of the law of motion of society and making a fetish of decisions which claim to be the incarnation of that law of motion — both were equally incom-patible with Gramsci's thinking.

---

[3] These theses were eventually published by Engels in 1888 as an appendix to his own book *Ludwig Feuerbach*. He says of them in his preface that they were: "notes hurriedly scribbled down for later elaboration and not intended for publication, but they are invaluable as the first document in which is deposited the brilliant germ of the new world outlook" — i.e. of historical materialism, or Marxism. (Trs.)

NATURE AND SOCIETY

Marx and Engels elaborated the idea of classical German philosophy that while hitherto the laws of social development have asserted themselves in a spontaneous and elemental way, now that men have lighted on their track they can consciously manipulate them. As regards the forms of society which have existed hitherto, this means that:

> "Although the totality of this movement appears as a social process, and although particular forces in this movement result from the conscious wills and various aims of individuals, the totality of the process appears as an objective connection which evolves spontaneously. It arises, it is true, from the conflicts between conscious individuals, but it does not lie within their consciousness nor, as a totality, is it subsumed under them. Their own conflict results in an alien social power confronting them; their interplay seems like a process and a force which is quite independent of them."[1]

It is the understanding of the process of development, therefore, which first makes it possible to intervene consciously in the workings of a necessity which then ceases to be alien and independent. Engels drew a parallel between social development asserting itself and advancing despite all accidents and retrogressions and Darwin's theory of development in which the products of nature are "the result of a long process of evolution."

> "But what is true of nature, which is hereby recognised also as a historical process of development, is also true of the history of society in all its branches ... Here, therefore, as in the realm of nature it is necessary ... to discover the general laws of motion which assert themselves as the ruling ones in the history of human society."[2]

True, he immediately follows this with the important qualification that: "In one point, however, the history of the development of society proves

---

[1] *Grundrisse der Politischen Ökonomie*, 1857 (Berlin, 1953) p. 111 (Outlines of Political Economy. Only one section of this work has been translated into English: *Pre-Capitalist Economic Formations*. (1964). Trs.)

[2] Engels: *Ludwig Feuerbach*, part iv.

to be essentially different from that of nature." In nature nothing happens as a consciously desired aim; but in history nothing happens without a conscious purpose, without a desired aim. But this distinction does not alter the fact that the course of history is also governed by inner general laws. For what is willed happens only rarely; consequently the conflict of innumerable individual wills and individual actions produces a state of affairs "which is entirely analogous to that which governs unconscious nature." For while the aim of the individual action is willed the result which follows from many individual actions is not willed, and ultimate by the outcome is consequences which are the different from the desired ones.

Engels returns to this thought in a letter to Bloch, dated 21st and 22nd September 1890, in a disquisiton on Marx's writings. He is both more flexible and more precise:

> "In the second place, however, history makes itself in such a way that the final result always arises from conflicts between many individual wills, of which each again has been made what it is by a host of particular conditions of life. Thus there are innumerable intersecting forces, an infinite series of parallelograms of forces which give rise to one resultant — the historical event. This again may itself be viewed as the product of a power which, taken as a whole, works *unconsciously* and without volition. For what each individual wills is obstructed by everyone else, and what emerges is something that no one willed. Thus past history proceeds in the manner of a natural process and is also essentially subject to the same laws of movement. But from the fact that individual wills — of which each desires what he is impelled to by his physical constitution and external, in the last resort economic, circumstances (either his own personal circumstances or those of society in general) — do not attain what they want, but are merged into a collective mean, a common resultant, it must not be concluded that their value = 0. On the contrary, each contributes to the resultant and is to this degree involved in it."

The comparison with the unconscious development of natural processes in accordance with natural laws remains unaltered, but the individual will and its contribution to the resultant 'parallelogram of forces' is given a more distinct emphasis. It is put even more clearly in a letter to Starkenberg, 25th January 1894:

> "Men make their history themselves, but not as yet with a collective will or according to a collective plan, nor even in a definitely defined,

given society. Their efforts clash and for that very reason all such societies are governed by necessity, which is supplemented by and appears under the form of accident."

Since, therefore, the law of motion of society works as objectively as a law of nature, men will readily realise that the transition to socialism can indeed be consciously brought about by men who understand that law. Men are placed in a form of society "which exists before they do, which they do not create, which is the product of the former generation".[3] By developing production — by living, that is — men develop social relations with each other whose form "necessarily" alters with the change and growth of the productive forces. Necessity arises from the activity of men who hitherto have, by and large, taken aim blindly. The socialist form of society is the first that is being deliberately fought for. Like every previous revolution it can only be accomplished by human beings; the new factor is that the forces that accomplish it are aware that their activity is occurring within the framework of a general law of development, namely the law of motion of history.

Capital "drives itself in its national economic movement towards its own dissolution — but only through a development which does not depend on it, of which it is unconscious and which takes place against its will, through the very nature of things, only inasmuch as it produces the proletariat as proletariat, the misery which is conscious of its spiritual and physical misery, the dehumanisation which, because it is conscious of its dehumanisation, will abolish it."[4]

The unity of the two concepts of objective development and proletarian revolution apparent in the youthful writings is also continued in Capital, which amongst other things holds fast to the idea that the concentration of capital sharpens the contradictions and antagonisms of the capitalist mode of production, "that is to say, it produces at one and the same time the elements for the formation of a new society and the forces for revolutionising the old one."[5]

And Karl Marx, the leader of the workers, expresses this concretely in a letter to Bolte of 23rd November 1871:

"The political movement of the working class has as its object, of course, the conquest of political power for the working class, and

[3] Marx in a letter to P. V. Annenkov, 28th Dec. 1846.
[4] Marx and Engels: The Holy Family (1845), Chapter 4.
[5] Marx: Capital. Vol. I Chap. 15, section 9 (concluding words).

for this it is naturally necessary that a previous organisation of the working class, itself arising from their economic struggles, should have been developed up to a certain point . . .

Where the working class is not yet far enough advanced in its organisation to undertake a decisive campaign against the collective power, i.e. the political power of the ruling classes, it must at any rate be trained for this by continual agitation against and a hostile attitude towards the policy of the ruling classes. Otherwise it will remain a plaything in their hands."

The Laws as Tendencies

From the very beginning Marx and Engels emphasised the peculiar character of social laws — including, therefore, the law of motion of history — by calling special attention to their character as tendencies.

"The general law asserts itself through the whole of capitalist production as the predominant tendency, but in a way which is always very complicated and approximate, as a never ascertainable average of perpetual fluctuations."[6]

And in the foreword to *Capital* Marx spoke of the laws as "tendencies working and asserting themselves with iron necessity". History deals with men who are endowed with wills and are faced with decisions. Consequently the working of the law inevitably results in counteracting factors which compensate for each other and cancel each other out, and in corresponding fluctuations. Therefore Marx was for ever stressing that in life as it is lived the law for various reasons gets corrected, modified and altered:

"In [describing] the theory it is assumed that the laws of the capitalist mode of production develop in a pure form. In reality there is always an approximation."[7]

And naturally, this is true also of the law of motion of all earlier modes of production.

[6] *Capital*. Vol. III, Chapter 9. Formation of a General Rate of Profit.
[7] *Ibid.* Chapter 10. Equalization of the General Rate of Profit through Competition.

Engels wrote about economic laws in a similar way in a letter to Conrad Schmidt, dated 12th March 1895:

> "And of economic laws in general — none of them has any reality except as approximation, tendency, average, and not as immediate reality. This is partly due to the fact that their action clashes with the simultaneous action of other laws, but partly to their own nature as concepts."

Marx and Engels took account of the complicated dialectic of recognised necessity and necessary recognition, of adherence to laws of development together with activity, when they were speaking of 'accidents' which can slow down or speed up the general pace of development — in connection, for example, with the role of personality in history. In a letter of 17th April 1871 Marx wrote to Kugelmann:

> "Making world history would indeed be very easy if the struggle were only taken up on the condition of infallibly favourable chances. On the other hand, it would be of a very mystical nature if 'accidents' played no part. These accidents themselves fall naturally into the general course of development and are compensated for again by other accidents. But the acceleration and retardation [of development] are very dependent on such 'accidents' — including the 'accident' of the character of the people who first stand at the head of the movement."

A Movement for the Eclipse of the Moon?

Marx and Engels never gave a coherent and detailed exposition of the chief problem of the Marxist conception of history, but in a number of passages they did deliberately emphasise 'necessity' and the comparison with processes of natural history. This has undoubtedly contributed to evoking the pretty speedy retort: If the transition to socialism is inevitable, where is the need for a movement to fight for socialism? After all, there is no movement to bring about the eclipse of the moon which will occur in (say) 1999.

Even leaving aside the eclipse of the moon, this extremely important objection is always cropping up. The French philosopher Jean Wahl makes the well-known comparison with religion:

> "The Christian is saved, but he must work, and help God ... Marxism is at one and the same time a description of the existing

state of affairs and a projection into the future . . . But history cannot be simultaneously already made and still needing to be made."[8]

And the German sociologist Rolf Dahrendorf argues in a similar vein:

"If communist society arises from dialectical necessity out of the contradictions of bourgeois society then that implies that it will come about quite independently of human understanding"[9]

But Dahrendorf is undoubtedly familiar with the famous passage in *Capital* in which understanding is dealt with as a part of social development, also with the passage in Engels' preface to *The Peasant War in Germany* where he insists on the proletariat's receptiveness to theoretical ideas and extols them therefore as the true heirs of classical philosophy. Knowledge, the decisions people make, morals, activity — they are all included in the law of social development. Historical materialism does not regard the business of a new form of society superseding an old one as a kind of relay race which can be timed by a stop-watch. Marxists are convinced of the necessity of capitalism being succeeded by socialism, but this conviction includes the certitude that this certitude will increasingly become the conviction of most men, especially of most working men. The appeal to moral obligation is not a denial of the idea that development follows certain laws which will be realised by men who decide the form and timing and rhythm of the working of these laws. It is impossible for men to go backwards from capitalism to feudalism, but they do decide how and in what way the transition to socialism shall come about; that *is* decided by them. Personal responsibility and moral obligation are not made superfluous thanks to some automatic conveyor belt; on the contrary, insight into the motive forces of human actions makes it possible for men to free themselves from a development where they suffer the fate described in Hölderlin's poem and for years, for centuries at a time, are tossed like spray from one rock to another and reach no certain goal.[10] In this connection one might perhaps suggest — other considerations will be examined later — a slight modification of Marx's thesis that the contradiction between the productive forces and property relations leads to periods of social

---

[8] *Quel Avenir Attend L'Homme*, Colloque de Royaumont, 17—20 May, 1961, p. 24.
[9] *Marx in Perspektive* (Berlin) p. 127.
[10] Hölderlin: 1770—1843. Romantic, highly individualist poet, near contemporary of Schiller; very sympathetic to the French Revolution. Eventually the isolation of the artist in capitalist society drove him mad. (Trs.)

revolution: it leads to periods of social crisis which are overcome by people making social revolutions.

Indeed, support for a modification of this kind can be found in several passages in Marx's writings dealing with the past and the interpretation of the past. History affords quite a few instances where the contradiction between the forces of production and the relations of production resulted in long periods of decadence and stagnation because the subjective factors needed to overcome the social crisis were missing.

Consequently it would certainly be no sort of sin against Marxism, but rather a correction in Marx's own spirit, if one were to dispense with one current formulation which, though supported by several passages in Marx and Engels, nonetheless seems to be a not altogether happy one. For example, in the *Political Economy* of the Polish economist Oskar Lange, we read:

> "Economic laws are the result of conscious purposeful activity by man, but all the same they possess a regularity which is independent of human wills and human consciousness ... because men carry on their affairs in definite social conditions and property relations."[11]

This is the traditional argument, faithful to the texts. In their economic activity men do indeed find that their bed is made ready for them (so to speak); they cannot choose the productive relations within which they live and earn their livelihood to suit themselves. Nevertheless, strictly speaking, one cannot characterise social laws, or even the main law of motion of society as being independent of the wills and consciousness of men. These laws do not correspond to this or that particular will and people cannot choose which new form of society shall stand on the historical order of the day; they have not even been aware that there is a law of development. But it is only because there are human wills, human consciousness and human activity that there can be any laws in the history of man and the development of human society.

A Comparison

The theory of the inevitability of the socialist revolution involves not only the idea of social development proceeding in accordance with certain laws (inevitability) but also the conviction that this has to be realised by

[11] First published in Warsaw in 1959. English translation (Pergamon Press) 1963, p. 227.

men — realised through a revolution. The law of motion of history is a law about human society; it can only operate through men. When, and how, depends upon the judgment and initiative of men who are themselves comprised within the law. Indeed, whether it operates at all depends ultimately on this: the advent of the atomic age has given a renewed actuality to Marx's alternatives: "either socialism or a descent into barbarism." The law of motion of society is no guarantee against the extermination of society.

The dialectical relationship between decisions of the human will and the law of social development ought to safeguard Marxism from the fatalistic degradation of that vulgar materialistic interpretation which it suffers at the hands of friend and foe alike. The contradiction between the productive forces and the relations of production finds expression in the class struggle, and the resolution of the contradiction ensues from the victory of the rising class. The recognition of the inevitability of socialism involves recognising that more and more people will recognise the necessity of this revolution. Therefore Marxism does not lead to a passive attendance upon an inevitable, automatic event; rather — as Lenin wrote in *Who the Friends of the People Are* — it is the foundation of rational action. The recognition that development proceeds in accordance with certain laws includes recognising that more and more people will be convinced of the necessity of this development. It is only because of this that the development becomes necessary. The development of history involves making efforts to win over increasing numbers of people as fighters for this development. One might well use the formulation Bertolt Brecht and say: "Things do not stay as they are. *You* must change them."

The objective law of development, operating as it does through the most varied and contradictory clashes of individual wishes and decisions, leaves plenty of scope for a quickening or slackening of the pace of what is broadly a certainty — plenty of scope for idiosyncrasies, deviations and uncertainties. It is not a kind of historical insurance policy or legal guarantee against defeats, setbacks and stagnation. It does not absolve anyone from moral responsibility or personal decision. It operates in a society of understanding, willing, active people, and it is realised through these people's understanding, wills and activity.

To what extent can one make a valid comparison between this and the conformity of nature to natural laws? Nowadays even Engels' example of the parallelogram of forces (which does correspond to the dialectical concept of social development conforming to certain laws) seems too rigid; it can only be understood in the context of the effort to bring out at all costs the new and revolutionary side of the Marxist conception of history. Comparisons with the laws of nature seem to us to-day acceptable only as analogies, and we reject any precise equations or equivalents.

Statisticians in insurance companies know that problems which are insoluble for an individual case taken on its own can, given a large number of cases, be solved in accordance with the theory of probability. In dealing with large numbers, accidents cancel each other out and there emerge interconnections, tendencies and necessary consequences. Gramsci protested against this comparison, which we have already met in Kant, on the ground that it degrades men to the level of passive individuals.[12] But since it still leaves each individual with his unique personality and power of decision the comparison seems to me justifiable. Here one may allow a certain parallel with several branches of the natural sciences. What is unobservable with regard to isolated particles does with large numbers yield mathematically calculable laws of probability. Quantity is transformed into quality, the accidental into the necessary, irregularity into order, the incalculable into an unambiguous development.

For example, thermodynamics is based on the fact that while no predictions can be made about the behaviour of individual molecules, nonetheless, where thousands of millions of molecules are involved, it is possible to establish statistical laws about them.

"Rather than investigating the dynamic laws governing one individual event, where we are still completely in the dark and there is no prospect of a tangible result, the first thing to do is to put together the observations made about a large number of individual events of a certain type and calculate means and averages from these. Then, according to the particular circumstances of the case, certain rules based on experience emerge from these averages; and the rules established in this way enable us to forecast the outcome of many future events — never with absolute certainty, granted, but with a probability which in practice comes very close to certainty; not in every detail, it is true, but in their average course. And this is what matters for most purposes."[13]

---

[12] A. Gramsci: *Il Materialismo Storico* p. 127.
[13] Max Planck: *Wege zur Physikalischen Erkenntnis* (Paths towards an Understanding of Physics.) Leipzig 1934; p. 53 (For Planck, c.f. Chapter 6, p. 57.)

Erwin Schroedinger pointed to a similar problem in modern atomic physics. From out of the "disorder" of the motion of fundamental particles the observation of a lot of particles yields "order". In a single milligram of radium forty million atoms explode every second; which ones, and why, we do not know. But we do know that after sixteen centuries half the milligram will have completely altered. Even the English physicist Eddington, who deduced as the principal conclusion from the results of modern physics that there is no knowledge, did allow that clear laws emerge for a large number of fundamental particles:

> "If the numbers involved are very large, chance is the best guarantee of certainty. Fortunately the study of molecules, energy and radiation does deal with a large number of particles and so we can achieve a degree of certainty which habitual players of roulette certainly do not attain".

The 'arbitrariness' of the individual instance is transformed by large numbers into probability and eventually into a law. Predictions which it is impossible to make about the behaviour of isolated cases because of the complexity and multiplicity of reciprocal effects become possible and unambiguous as the number of objects increases, even if the objects are subjects. In dealing with a large number the distinction between certainty and ascertainability, which plays a large part in the philosophical discussions of modern natural science, becomes unimportant.

Several of the characteristic features of cybernetics also make it possible to draw a certain analogy between the natural and the social sciences. Cybernetics deals with dynamic self-regulating systems which, by means of a system of feedback, are able to cancel out accidents, oscillations and fluctuations. They are adjusted to a certain target and a definite programme, and the arrangement for the transmission of signals and feedback then ensures that there is no disturbance. It seems to me that the comparison made by the Austrian scholar Wolfgang Wieser when he discusses this system in his book *Organisms, Structures and Machines*,[14] is a valid one — even though the concepts that he uses seem to me mistaken. For he sees "the unpredictability of the electron, the unpredictability of nervous impulses and probably even the unpredictability of human actions within a

---

[14] *Organismen, Strukturen, Maschinen* p. 84 (Fischer-Bücherei, n. d.).

social system" as having a dual aspect: irregularity in each individual part, order in the whole.

Like many men of science, Wieser sees in indeterminism the impossibility of making any exact predictions. This does apply to isolated particles but ceases to be true of the "order" which involves many particles, a whole system of particles. While being cautious about making comparisons between different disciplines, it is permissible to regard the mode of production and the law governing its development as a dynamic system in which fluctuations, oscillations and disturbances are in the last resort overcome by the dynamism of the system.

Men make their own history, but under conditions which they cannot arrange to suit themselves. Consequently their free-will consists of a freedom to choose, in which the motives governing their choices are socially and historically determined, even if people feel that they have arrived at them freely. The laws governing the development of society have operated hitherto more or less blindly, going against and beyond men's wishes and efforts. But men can speed up this development if their wishes and efforts are in accord with its spirit. Thus appeals to morality and personal responsibility do not stand in contradiction to an understanding of the laws of social development: they are part and parcel of those laws.

Marx' and Engels' understanding of the objective laws of development of human society did not cause them to abandon the concept which they had already adopted in their early work *The Holy Family*:

> "History does nothing, it 'possesses no immense wealth', it 'wages no battles'. It is man, real living man, that does all that, that possesses and fights; 'history' is not a person apart, using man as a means for its own particular aims; history is nothing but the activity of man pursuing his aims."[15]

And it is in this very same *Holy Family* that we read of the need for the socialist revolution and the necessary role of the proletariat in that revolution:

> "Indeed private property, too, drives itself in its national economic movement towards its own dissolution but only through a development which does not depend on it, of which it is unconscious and which takes place against its will, through the very nature of things,

[15] Marx and Engels: *The Holy Family*, Chapter 6.

only inasmuch as it produces the proletariat as proletariat, the misery which is conscious of its spiritual and physical misery, the dehumanisation which because it is conscious of its dehumanisation will abolish it. The proletariat executes the sentence that private property pronounces on itself by producing the proletariat, just as it executes the sentence that wage-labour pronounces on itself by producing wealth for others and misery for itself . . .

When socialist writers ascribe this historic role to the proletariat, it is not because they consider the proletarians as gods. It is rather the other way round. Since the loss of all humanity, even semblance of humanity, is practically complete in the fully developed proletariat; since the conditions of life of the proletariat sum up all the conditions of life in society today in their most inhuman form; since man has lost himself in the proletariat, but at the same time has not only gained theoretical consciousness of that loss, but is driven through imperative needs which can no longer be refused or palliated — through the practical expression of necessity — to revolt against that inhumanity; therefore the proletariat can and must free itself. But it cannot free itself without abolishing the conditions of its own life, without abolishing all the inhuman conditions of life of society today which are summed up in its situation. Not in vain does it go through the stern but steeling school of labour. It is not a question of what this or that proletarian, or even the whole of the proletariat at the moment, considers as its aim. It is a question of what the proletariat is, and what, in conformity with that being, it will be historically compelled to do. Its aim and historical action is irrevocably and clearly indicated in its own life situation as well as in the whole organisation of bourgeois society today. There is no need to dwell here upon the fact that a large part of the English and French proletariat is already conscious of its historic task and is constantly working to develop that consciousness into complete clarity."[16]

In this passage (as writers on Marx often stress) Marx is not dealing with the basic contradiction; as the Jesuit writer Calvez points out in his book on Marx,[17] what is being dealt with here is the fundamental idea of Marxist dialectics, the chief problem of the Marxist conception of history.

[16] *Ibid.* Chapter 4.
[17] S. Y. Calvez, *Karl Marx*, pp. 372—3.

The passage just quoted concludes by seizing on consciousness and conscious activity as the immanent part of necessity. It is the same idea as we find in the youthful Marx's third thesis on Feuerbach:

"The coincidence of the changing of circumstances and of human activity can only be comprehended and rationally understood as revolutionary practice."

6

INTERVENTION WITH ECHOES

The 'natural historical' side of the law of motion of society, and consequently of the transition to socialism, which was often emphasised in the classical writers, became even more 'natural historical' amongst their successors — on the one hand as a justification of passivity and opportunism, and on the other as a stimulus to activity, even to the point of glorifying subjective voluntarism. Historical determinism took on a fatalistic tinge. As interpreted by Kautsky it reverted to the mechanical materialism criticised by Marx in his *Theses on Feuerbach*, which understands reality only as an object of contemplation, but not as sensuous human activity and praxis. It is no accident that the characters in Kautsky's historical writings have about as much life in them as pressed flowers. Or take the concrete examples given by Plekhanov in his study of the role of the individual in history, such as the example of Napoleon borrowed from Engels and vulgarised by Plekhanov, which Sartre so rightly criticises. These come pretty close to a fatalistic view of history, though here of course one must make allowances for the fact that Plekhanov had to argue with those Narodniks[1] who regarded history simply as the work of individual heroes, so that he was obliged to stress the scientific standpoint of the Marxist approach to history.

It is a remarkable thing, therefore, and yet typical, that during the period of the so-called cult of personality (which ascribed all achievements to a single individual) Plekhanov's works came to be given a quite undue reverence in the Soviet Union although he had been one of the most determined opponents of the Bolsheviks. It is evidence of the extent to which the "Marxism—Leninism" of the Stalin epoch managed to combine the fatalistic interpretation of the Marxist view of history with a subjective voluntarism: naked arbitrariness donned the majestic robes of those inescapable universal laws.

---

[1] Narodniks (Russian Narod = people). The main group in opposition to the Tsar's autocratic government in Russia in the 1880s. Ignoring the growth of industrialisation and the working class, they held that the peasant commune gave the basis for socialism, and sought to overthrow the existing government by individual acts of terrorism (e.g. the assassination of Alexander II in 1881). (Trs.)

Along with this soulless, fatalistic interpretation of the Marxist view of history went a corresponding impoverishment of Marxist historical writing. Frederick Engels had already uttered a warning against employing concepts and ideas as a substitute for the concrete study of real historical facts. Men make their history in the circumstances in which they find themselves, but they are not mechanical puppets and the laws of social development only assert themselves as general tendencies. The vulgarised Marxist historical writing which dominated the scene in the Soviet Union from the thirties onwards dissolved all colour, character and subtlety in concepts and ideas. Personalities, contradictions and accidental happenings which threatened to burst the bounds of these concepts and ideas were ignored as being either uninteresting or non-existent. And at the same time a certain idiom was developed which explained every detail and the shape things took by reference to the general laws of history: every error and accident was represented as being either inevitable and absolutely necessary — or else as irrelevant anyway. Historians forgot Marx's *Eighteenth Brumaire*,[2] and the politicians practised the methods of the historians.

Measures taken in this or that province were represented as being an expression of conformity to a process governed by objective laws, and to every juridical law was assigned the infallibility of an objective law of nature — so that it often happened that some law which had been proclaimed as objectively necessary was accepted later on, after self-criticism, as having been subjectively erroneous and objectively superfluous. Certainly, in the countries which they are leading, Marxists must try to build the new socialist society on the foundations of a clear insight into what forces promote social development; but this approach only serves to give the general direction, not every little turning; it does for the broad perspective but not for every particular moment.

For example, it is certainly legitimate to consider the change-over to co-operative farming as an element in the development of socialism. But to proclaim this as the expression of an objective law at the very moment it was decreed, (as happened several times), as if it were not individual men but general world-wide laws which were responsible for the decree and

---

[2] *The Eighteenth Brumaire of Louis Bonaparte* (1852). A study of the 1848 revolution in France and the subsequent seizure of power by the future Napoleon III. Generally considered the finest example of Marx's application of his own historical method; while giving a thorough analysis of the class forces involved, it also gives full weight to the influence of personality and devotes most space to the details of the political battles and a description of those engaged in them (Trs.)

its timing, is evidence of a soulless, fatalistic interpretation of the Marxist view of history.

In his last work, *Economic Problems of Socialism in the U.S.S.R.* (1952), Stalin invented a so-called objective law about the planned and balanced development of the economy under socialism. That the socialisation of the means of production opens up the possibility of a planned and balanced development of the economy seems certain. But this possibility does not amount to an objective law about it. The disproportions (some great, some small) in the economies of those countries which have abolished the capitalist ownership of the means of production have furnished and are furnishing ample proof of this. That did not prevent wishful thinking being proclaimed as a law. And where violations of this "law" occurred it was attributed to violations of actual juridical laws.

Sartre's Polemic.

The mechanical vulgarisation of the Marxist philosophy of history led to an intervention whose echoes have not yet died away, but which would probably not have been necessary if Gramsci's contribution had been known and heeded. Sartre has attempted a synthesis between Marxism and existentialism.[3] He justifies this by saying that he has set himself the task of re-introducing into Marxist thought and into the universality of its concepts "the unsurpassable individuality of the human adventure", and of "creating within the framework of Marxism a genuinely comprehensive knowledge which will rediscover man in society and follow him in his praxis" — taking as its starting-point the dialectical character of individual actions, which consists in the fact "that man undergoes the dialectic as much as he makes it, and makes it as much as he undergoes it."[4] According to "the rotten Marxists" (Sartre says), Marx's lazy successors, man is the unresisting product, the sum of conditioned reflexes, because his make-up is entirely determined by existing circumstances, which means ultimately by economic conditions. The Marxist criticism of the thesis of mechanical materialism — to say that men are simply the products of their circum-

[3] See note on Kierkegaard, Chapter I p. 15. But Sartre's existentialism is secular, not religious. (Trs.)

[4] J. P. Sartre, *Critique de la Raison Dialectique* (Paris, 1960) pp. 108, 111, 131. The first part of this work has been translated by Hazel Barnes under the title of *The Problem of Method* (1964). See her pages 176, 181. (Trs.)

stances is to forget that it is precisely men who change circumstances — this (Sartre says) has been forgotten. Out of the understanding that men make their history in certain given circumstances there has come to be left only the circumstances. However, really it is not the previous contents of history but men who make history, otherwise men would merely be the vehicles of inhuman forces which are directing social development through them.

Sartre, however, does not dispute that actions and decisions are socially conditioned, or that the end result of the sum total of human activity presents itself to men as an alien force, as a chain of "compelling forces by which we are subjugated". But for him the point is to affirm the specific character of the human act *(l'acte humain)* "which holds fast to its resolves while traversing the social scene *(milieu)* and which, on the basis of given conditions, transforms the world". Within a certain field of possibilities man steps outside his historical and social limitations "by what he succeeds in making of what has been made of him". This overstepping of one's own social and historical limitations Sartre calls "the project".

> "It is indeed by reaching beyond the given into the field of the possible, and bringing one of all the many possibilities to realisation, that the individual achieves his objectivisation and makes a contribution to history. For it is then that his project achieves a reality which perhaps the agent may not perceive but which, through the conflicts which it reveals and generates, influences the course of events."[5]

Thus Sartre, just like Gramsci, opposes the attempt to understand the historical process simply as the mean between opposing forces and he also rejects Engels' picture of the parallelogram of forces; but in so doing he quite forgets Engels' important observation that every individual action is comprised in what results from it; and he leaves unanswered the problem of why it is, then, that there are general laws of history and forms of society.

On the whole, it seems to me that this is the decisive weakness of Sartre's synthesis. His polemic against the vulgar form of Marxism which swamps the doings of the individual man with his needs and sufferings and strivings — his "existence" to use Sartre's term — in general concepts; which loses sight of the impulse derived from choosing alternatives "from amongst the field of possibilities" in general laws; which because of the thesis that men make history within the limitations of certain given circumstances

[5] Sartre, op. cit. pp. 63, 64. (Hazel Barnes p. 91)

forgets the actual men and that it is they who make history — this part of the polemic was a wholesome antidote to the deadening of the Marxist philosophy of history. The endeavour "to restore man to his proper place within Marxism" was a salutary one. True, in the course of doing this, Sartre exaggerated the anaemic quality of contemporary Marxism, he vulgarized Engels, and Marx he occasionally misunderstood altogether.[6] But that seems to me less important than his salutary protest against the deadening of Marxism. That deserves our respect, for Marxism is a philosophy of action, and not simply a philosophy of interpretation.

Polemic with Sartre

Thus while the Polish philosopher Adam Schaff is right when he reproaches Sartre for often forgetting, when he talks about the singularity of human behaviour, that human existence is "an ensemble of social relations" (as Marx put it in his Theses on Feuerbach), he does Sartre an injustice, to my mind, when he accuses him of forgetting the specific dialectic of human history "which is inherent in understanding the individual as both the product and at the same time the maker of society". For that is the very foundation of Sartre's attempt, which seems all the more justified when we find that even Schaff will use such a formula as this:

> "The statement that people make their own history on the basis of given circumstances leads not to a denial of historical determinism but rather to a specific interpretation of the mechanism by which that determinism operates."[7]

[6] Sartre felt that he could adduce in support of his views the passage in the preface to the Critique of Political Economy where Marx wrote that "Just as our opinion of an individual is not based on what he thinks of himself so we cannot judge a period of transformation by its own consciousness..." Thus Marx also (Sartre said) stressed the heterogeneity of human knowledge and praxis, and recognised that they exist on different planes and that praxis cannot be exhausted and explained by knowledge. But in relying on these words of Marx Sartre was too hasty, because the passage quoted goes on to say: "...this consciousness must rather be explained from the contradictions of material life, from the existing conflict between the social forces of production and the relations of production." Apparently Sartre felt specially uneasy about the word 'explained'. But really Marx here was simply emphasising the need to discover the decisive motive forces in social development which lie behind the illusions, fancies and ideas of classes and periods.

[7] Adam Schaff: A Philosophy of Man (London, 1965) pp. 40, 42.

Here indeed determinism really is seen as a kind of mechanism "which has been imported into this all-embracing philosophy from outside."[8]

Sartre does not deny that the range of possibilities for human activity is socially conditioned. He also accepts Marx's view that the contradiction between the forces of production and the relations of production leads to an epoch of social revolution — and consequently he accepts the law of motion of history as containing the socialist future. It is precisely in this field of possibilities that he sees the possibility of giving meaning to social activity. But he ties himself up in a string of contradictions, in my opinion, when he proclaims the primacy of doing over knowing, and stresses the profound qualitative difference which separates the individual quality of existence from knowing and understanding. For by so doing he fails to answer the question: Why then are there certain general laws in history, distinct periods and forms of society? — something that he does not directly dispute. Why do certain predominant trends assert themselves above the strife of different conflicting wills? Undoubtedly in vulgar Marxist writings the force of the impulse of individual action (praxis) and personal choice has often been lost sight of, but in Sartre's synthesis it is often the basic idea of the Marxist science of history which gets overlooked. Perhaps (as Simone de Beauvoir relates in her autobiography, which also deals with Sartre) this is all bound up with that attitude of Sartre's which made him unwilling to reduce the difference between colours to the different wavelengths of electromagnetic impulses.

For the problem posed in this book Sartre's intervention has a double importance. His examination of the basic tenets of the Marxist view of history produced a useful swing of the pendulum against the fatalistic view of the law-governed character of the process of development; he raised the problem of free-will and freedom of decision to a new level, following (as I see it) a specific tradition in philosophy. Diderot had already — in a letter of 29th June 1756 — uttered a warning against "de confondre le volontaire avec le libre" (against confusing an act which is willed with a free act). There can be no action, no act of will, without a motive, or which is not circumscribed by social organisation, by upbringing and by a whole chain of circumstances. Consequently man's will is not free; it can be influenced and changed. And therein lies (said Diderot) the value of good

[8] Sartre: *Critique de la raison dialectique* p. 108 (Hazel Barnes p. 175)

example, of education and of social laws: "they can change men's pliable wills." *(The Dream of d'Alembert)*. Already here we catch a glimpse of the Marxist dialectic: circumstances affect men, but also men alter circumstances.

On the foundations laid by Kant, Schopenhauer (1788—1860) established both "the complete and stern necessity" of an act of the will and also "consciousness of the arbitrariness and primitiveness" which accompany it. He called in aid the distinction drawn by Kant: in the world of appearances we have the strict causality and necessity of acts of the will; but in humanity's being and essence there lies freedom and we become conscious of it through the exercise of responsibility. Man operates through stern necessity; but he is what he is by virtue of freedom. In this connection Franz Mehring[9] has popularised amongst Marxists the famous example of water. Water can break in waves, it can plunge down a waterfull, and it can leap into the air in a jet and evaporate. In certain conditions it can do all this; but it just so happens that it stays "of its own free-will" in a quiet pond. And Mehring draws a parallel with the citizen who of an evening has the chance to start doing all kinds of things, to go out if he wants to, but it just so happens that he goes home to his wife — "of his own free-will". Mehring was very fond of this example as illustrating the concrete problem of free-will within the limits of a determinist conception. But the dialectic of the problem (which we have already seen appearing in Diderot) escaped him in that he only quoted one side, the determinist side, of Schopenhauer's ideas.

Planck, the originator of the quantum theory, tackled the problem after Schopenhauer in the light of natural science. From an objective scientific point of view (he said) the human will is determined; from a subjective point of view, from the standpoint of self-consciousness, the human will is free. The will of a stranger, the will of our fellow-men, strikes us as being determined; our own only seems so *post factum*. However, what is willed in the present and the future cannot be considered as being pre-

[9] F. Mehring 1846—1919. Born of a well-to-do Pomeranian family but always an outspoken opponent of Prussian militarism, in 1890 he joined the German Social-Democratic Party and contributed to Kautsky's *Neue Zeit*. Unlike Kautsky, however, he stayed true to his principles and was imprisoned for his opposition to the 1914 war. He joined Rosa Luxemburg in forming the Spartacus League. Besides many brilliant essays of Marxist literary criticism on Goethe and others he wrote the classic biography of Marx (1918; translated into English by Edward Fitzgerald 1936.) (Trs.)

determined. Like most physicists who go in for philosophy, Planck here is making the mistake of equating "determined" with "determinable".

In all these earlier random examples from the history of philosophy we find the same philosophical problem that Sartre lays before Marxists: the interaction of man and his environment, of freedom and helplessness, of 'project' with social and historical conditions. Man acts and takes decisions within a range of possibilities which is already there confronting him independently of him; but he has a choice of decisions. His choice, his project, oversteps the conditions and preserves them while creating new conditions.

> "What do we really mean by making history under pre-existing circumstances? ... My formulation, which has been inspired by Marx's ideas, is simply a reminder that man makes history to exactly the same extent as history makes him ... Because man only exists for man in certain definite social circumstances and conditions, every human relationship is a historical one. But historical relationships are human to the extent that they are at all times the direct dialectical result of praxis, that is to say, of the plurality of activities within a single field of practice."[10]

In his polemic with "rotten Marxism" in which all law and all necessity is cast-iron and inflexible, Sartre put all the emphasis he could on decisions of the will, the possibility of alternatives and personal responsibility. So it is all the more surprising that he never entered into any discussion of what seems to me the chief problem of the theory of revolution, namely, that the Marxist law of motion of society has been realised in ways different from that foreseen by Marx and Engels. The fact that it was necessary to replace Marx's theory of revolution with a new one, the Leninist theory of revolution, has thrown fresh light on the dialectic of the main philosophical problem of the Marxist conception of history: how to understand the relationship between social development which conforms to certain laws and the decisions which men choose to make, the relation of objective inner laws to subjective possibilities and capabilities — and then, having understood this, how to act upon it.

[10] Sartre, *Critique de la raison dialectique*, p. 180.

THE MATURING OF THE MATERIAL CONDITIONS
FOR THE SOCIALIST REVOLUTION

The term socialist revolution is used here (and throughout this essay) to mean the transfer of the means of production to social ownership. I am well aware — as indeed with the practical experience of building socialism increasing numbers of people have become aware — that this does not exhaust the meaning of the socialist revolution, still less of the construction of socialism. Nonetheless, this remains the basic fact of socialist revolution, especially when (as in this case) the revolution is being considered from the point of view of the law of motion of history.

In the first place, this way of looking at things enables us to understand the material preconditions of the socialist revolution, namely, the increasing contradiction between the social character of the forces of production and the private appropriation of the products, between the expansion of the forces of production and the limits which they find themselves up against in the relations of production, the property relations. Marx and Engels were always stressing that both the social character of production and also concentration and monopolisation in the ownership of the means of production and in the appropriation of the product constantly increase, and that consequently there is also a constant sharpening of those contradictions which set free the impulses that overturn the old society and the elements that go to shape the new one. As the most extreme expression of these contradictions they pointed to the cyclical economic crises which hasten the concentration of capital and by enlarging the industrial reserve army also produce the pauperism which Marx considered to be essential to the general law of capitalist accumulation. It was principally in his early works, in the *Communist Manifesto* and *Wage-Labour and Capital* (1849), that Marx asserted that these cyclical economic crises get more severe each time. And it was chiefly after the defeat of the 1848 revolution that he expressed the view that the revolution would only be possible as the result of a new crisis — which was just as certain to occur, however, as the present one. These opinions of Marx's about economic crises getting more severe and more widespread each time and their being the prelude to revolution were really taken to heart by the revolutionary working-class movement and learned as basic tenets of scientific socialism as a result of the great economic crisis of 1929.

To my mind the most significant description of the material preconditions of the socialist revolution is contained in Volume Three of *Capital*:

"The real barrier to capitalist production is capital itself; it is the fact that capital and its utilisation appear to be the start and the finish, the motive and aim of production. Production is just production for capital, instead of its being the other way round, with the means of production being simply the means whereby the society of producers can shape an ever fuller life for themselves. The limits within which the preservation and realisation of the value of capital have to operate, depending upon the expropriation and impoverishment of the great mass of the producers — these limits constantly come into conflict with the methods of production which capital has to employ for its own purposes and which steer straight towards an unlimited increase in production, towards production as an end in itself, towards an unconditional development of the productive forces of society. The means — unconditional development of the productive forces of society — constantly comes into conflict with the limited end of the utilisation of the capital available. Thus while the capitalist mode of production is historically a means for developing the productive forces and creating a world market to correspond, at the same time there is a constant conflict between this historic task and the corresponding social relations of production."[1]

Economic crises give expression to this contradiction and bring it to a head.

"The ultimate cause of all real crises is always the poverty and restricted consumption of the masses in contrast to the urge of capitalist production to develop the productive forces as if society's absolute capacity for consumption were their limit."[2]

The Evidence is Already Available in Capitalism

Marx also pointed out in *Capital* that the social character of production and the basic expansion of the productive forces already, within capitalist society, provide indications which show that capitalism is obsolete within

[1] *Capital* Vol. III Chap. 15: Unravelling the Internal Contradictions of the Law.
[2] *Ibid*, Chapter 30: Money Capital and Actual Capital.

its lifetime. Marx saw limited companies as an expression of the enormous expansion in the scale of production and as undertakings which are too large for the individual capitalist:

> "Capital which rests on a social mode of production and which presupposes a social concentration of the means of production and the forces of labour here acquires directly the form of social capital (the capital of individuals who are directly associated) in contrast to private capital, and its enterprises come into being as social enterprises in contrast to private enterprises. It is the abolition of capital as private property within the bounds of the capitalist mode of production itself."[3]

Within the limits of the capitalist mode of production the capitalist is already becoming a "superfluous person" in the production process; the job of superintending and directing things can be left to managers; the social function becomes divorced from the appropriation of the surplus labour of others.

> "This result of the highest development of capitalist production is a necessary transition to the reconversion of capital into the property of the producers, no longer as the private property of individual producers but as the common property of associates, as directly social property. On the other hand it is a transition to the conversion of all the functions in the process of reproduction, hitherto bound up with capitalist private property, into simple functions of the associated producers, into social functions."[4]

Engels, who saw to the publication of Volume Three of *Capital*, inserted a note here saying that since Marx had written these words new forms of industrial enterprise had developed representing the second and third degrees of joint stock companies, viz. cartels on a national and on an international scale. "But even this form of the socialisation of production was still insufficient." In some particular branches of production, Engels went on, the entire production was put under the direction of a trust, as for example in the case of the English United Alkali Trust:

> "So in England in this branch of production which forms the basis of the whole chemical industry, competition has been replaced by

---

[3] *Ibid*, Chapter 27: The Role of Credit in Capitalist Production.
[4] *Ibid*.

monopoly, so paving the way very nicely for future expropriation by the whole of society, by the nation."[5]

Here Engels, like Marx, confines himself to depicting the objective, economic, material conditions of the revolution, which indeed eventually release the subjective factors also. Marx goes on to say:

"Here we have the abolition of the capitalist mode of production within the capitalist mode of production itself, and consequently a self-destructive contradiction which presents itself *prima facie* simply as the point of transition to a new form of production. It manifests its contradictory nature by its effects. It establishes monopoly in certain spheres and so provokes the intervention of the state."[6]

And in the Gotha programme of the German Social-Democratic Party, as also in Marx's criticism of the programme (1875), we meet the idea that "the present capitalist society eventually creates the material conditions which fit, indeed force, the workers to break that social curse" which culminates in the increasing poverty and suffering of the workers. Engels carried on this thought in *Socialism, Utopian and Scientific*. There too economic crises are presented as the strongest proof that the mode of production rebels against the mode of exchange, and that capitalism has become incapable of controlling the developing forces of production. It is formulated like a law of nature:

"And on the other hand these productive forces themselves press forward with increasing force to put an end to the contradiction, to rid themselves of their character as capital, to the actual recognition of their character as social productive forces."[7]

That is one side of it. But on the other side Engels immediately goes on in this passage to make the point — so often overlooked in the 'folklore' presentation of the Marxist conception of history — that the capitalist class, too, is capable of taking these material developments into account:

"It is this pressure of the productive forces, in their mighty up-growth, against their character as capital, increasingly compelling the recognition of their social character, which forces the capitalist class

[5] *Ibid*.
[6] *Ibid*.
[7] Section iii.

itself more and more to treat them as social productive forces, in so far as this is at all possible within the framework of capitalist relations."[8]

Here (as in his interpolation in Volume Three of *Capital*, already quoted) Engels is referring to the new "forms of the socialisation of great masses of the means of production" met with in the joint stock companies. "At a certain stage of development even this form no longer suffices" and trusts are created — unions "for the purpose of regulating production" — and finally the "still greater concentration of association", the monopolies.

> "In the trusts free competition is transformed into monopoly; the unplanned production of capitalist society capitulates before the planned production of the invading socialist society. At first, certainly, still to the benefit and advantage of the capitalists. But here the exploitation is so obvious that it must collapse. No nation would put up with production conducted by trusts, with such a barefaced exploitation of the community by a tiny band of coupon-clippers *(Kuponabschneidern)*."[9]

Again and again, as a corollary to this inevitable development, he draws the revolutionary conclusion from this development, as something equally inevitable. Eventually, (he says) in several branches of the economy such as the major means of communication, like the postal and telegraph services and the railways, even these forms of socialisation prove to be insufficient. "In one way or another, whether with trusts or without, ultimately the official representative of capitalist society, the state, is obliged to take over the direction of production." This nationalisation, where it has become economically inevitable, signifies "an economic advance, the attainment of another step preliminary to the taking over of all productive forces by society itself". If economic crises signify the incapacity of the bourgeoisie for any further management of the productive forces, then nationalisation demonstrates "that the bourgeoisie can be dispensed with for this purpose". The capitalist no longer has any social function to perform; he has become superfluous. Acts of nationalisation by the capitalist state certainly do not abolish the capitalist relationship, but they carry it to an extreme. State ownership of the productive forces is not the solution to the great social conflict between the character of the productive forces

[8] *Ibid.*
[9] *Ibid.*

and the private ownership of the means of production, but it contains within itself the formal means, the key, to the solution.

"This solution can only consist in the recognition in practice of the social nature of the modern productive forces, in bringing, therefore, the mode of production, appropriation and exchange into harmony with the social character of the means of production. And this can only be brought about by society openly and directly taking possession of the productive forces which have outgrown all control other than that of society itself. Thereby the social character of the means of production and of the products — which today operates against the producers themselves, periodically breaking through the mode of production and exchange and asserting itself only as a blind law of nature, violently and destructively — will be quite consciously utilised by the producers, and transformed from a cause of disorder and periodic collapse into the most powerful lever of production itself."[10]

Instead of productive anarchy there will be social direction of production according to a plan, corresponding to the needs of the whole people and of each individual. Proletarian state power completes this transformation — a transformation which has already been forced on and brought to economic maturity within the relationships of capitalism.

The Eve of Socialism

On the eve of the October revolution, in a period when the maturing of the material conditions for a socialist revolution as indicated by Marx and Engels had taken on an even more extreme form, with the social character of production intensified, especially in the state monopoly capitalism of the war economy — at that juncture Lenin drew special attention once again to the significance of this development. In his pamphlet The Threatening Catastrophe and How to Avoid it, written in September 1917, we read:

"For socialism is nothing but the next step forward from state capitalist monopoly. In other words, socialism is nothing but state capitalist monopoly made to serve the interests of the whole people; and thereby it ceases to be capitalist monopoly.

[10] Ibid.

64

There is no middle course here. The objective course of development is such that it is impossible to advance from monopolies (whose number, role and importance have been increased tenfold by the war) without advancing towards socialism."

And again:

"The dialectics of history are such that the war, having accelerated the transformation of monopoly capitalism into state monopoly capitalism, has by the same token brought humanity immeasurably closer to socialism . . .

. . . because state monopoly capitalism is the fullest material preparation for socialism, is its threshold, is that rung on the ladder of history between which and the rung called socialism there are no intermediate rungs, . . .

"In reality socialism looks at us now through all the windows of present-day capitalism; the outline appears before us in practice; it emerges from every important measure forming a step forward on the basis of this modern capitalism."[11]

Lenin's arguments might be taken simply as a continuation of Marx' and Engels' ideas on the material prerequisites of a socialist revolution, taking account also of the growth towards state monopoly capitalism, were it not that Marx and Engels put forward the conception that the socialist revolution, in accordance with its material prerequisites, would be victorious first in the industrially advanced countries — since, as Marx put it in the famous preface to the *Critique of Political Economy*, no form of society ever disappears before all its productive forces have been developed, and new higher relations of production never take its place before the material conditions for their existence have matured in the womb of the old society. For that reason Marx wrote in a confidential communication of the General Council of the International Working Men's Association in January 1870 that despite the weaknesses of the English working-class movement England, as the metropolis of capitalism, was the decisive country in the international working-class movement. "Even though the revolutionary initiative is apparently starting in France only England can serve as the lever of a serious economic revolution." "It is the country", the document went on, "where there is no longer any peasantry; where

[11] Collected Works Vol. 25 pp. 358—9.

almost the whole of production has now been brought within the capitalist framework; where the great majority of the population are wage-earners; where the material conditions for the abolition of large private estates and of capitalism have developed furthest; and where the class struggle and the organisation of the working class in trade unions are widespread and have attained a certain degree of maturity." "The English possess all the necessary material prerequisites of the socialist revolution. What they lack is the spirit of generalisation and revolutionary passion. Only the General Council can instil this into them and so hasten the coming of a genuinely revolutionary movement in this country — and consequently everywhere else."[12]

Once more, the problems of practical politics bring us face to face with the basic problem of the Marxist conception of history. The law can only be realised through human beings; the maturing of the material conditions for the socialist revolution does not determine the maturity of the spiritual conditions for the socialist revolution; the economic law of motion of history only makes headway if enough people are set in motion.

And indeed this occurred first of all in backward Russia, in a country which did not fit the model of the Marxist law of motion. That was Lenin's great achievement, that he foresaw the possibility of this happening. He modified the Marxist theory of revolution by fastening on certain ideas which were already to be found in Marx and Engels despite the model, or rather, on the border of the model.

[12] **Marx**—Engels Ausgewählte Werke (Munich 1962) p. 1115.

8

THE MODIFICATION OF THE LAW

In the *Communist Manifesto* we find this significant passage:

> "The Communists turn their attention chiefly to Germany, because
> that country is on the eve of a bourgeois revolution that is bound to be
> carried out under more advanced conditions in European civilisation
> and with a more developed proletariat than that of England in the
> 17th and of France in the 18th century, and consequently the bourgeois
> revolution in Germany can be but the immediate prelude to a pro-
> letarian revolution."[1]

The idea was destined to be an important one, a practical modification
of the general law that it is the expansion of the productive forces which
leads to an epoch of social revolution. A country can come to the forefront
of revolutionary attention and revolutionary events because it is — backward. And the reserve forces of the bourgeois revolution can improve the
prospects of a socialist revolution.

After the 1848 revolution Marx and Engels applied these reflections to
backward Russia. But their relevance to Germany also is indicated in a
famous passage in a letter written by Marx to Engels on 16th April 1856 in
which he upheld the view that the unresolved tasks of the bourgeois
revolution could be solved by a proletarian revolution and so hasten that on:

> "The whole thing in Germany will depend on the possibility of
> backing the proletarian revolution by some second edition of the
> Peasants' War."

As regards Russia's prospects, Marx and Engels were principally concerned with the problem of whether the communal ownership among the
peasantry would be destroyed by the development of capitalism or whether
it could, at a higher level, facilitate and hasten the development of socialism.
Writing in 1875 on *Social Relations in Russia* Engels held that the second
course would only be possible "if, before the complete break-up of communal ownership, a proletarian revolution is successfully carried out in

[1] *Communist Manifesto*, Section iv.

Western Europe, creating for the Russian peasant the pre-conditions requisite for such a transition, particularly the material conditions which he needs if only to carry through the revolution (necessarily connected therewith) of his whole agricultural system." Opposing the view, widely held in Russia at that time, that Russia was nearer to a socialist revolution than the workers of Western Europe, Engels said that Russian communal ownership could only be saved by a proletarian revolution in the West. True, Russia was standing on the eve of a revolution, but certainly not a socialist one. "Started by the upper classes of the capital, perhaps even by the government itself, if it is to be carried further, and got quickly beyond the first constitutional phase, it will have to be through the peasants."[2]

In the preface to the Russian edition of the *Communist Manifesto* (21st January 1882) Marx and Engels were more explicit. They called Russia "the vanguard of revolutionary activity in Europe" and underlined the possibility of the communal ownership of the villages passing straight over into communist common ownership. But at the same time they also pointed out that the proletarian revolution would occur first in the West, in accordance with the law of motion of history which they had worked out:

> "If the Russian revolution becomes the signal for a proletarian revolution in the West, so that both complement each other, the present Russian common ownership of land may serve as the starting point for a communist development."

Obviously underlying these words was the conviction that it was the industrially advanced countries of Western Europe which would be the setting for the socialist revolution. But because Russia (to which Marx and Engels at times devoted their chief attention) would have to solve the problems of a bourgeois revolution in more advanced conditions than England in the seventeenth or France in the eighteenth century, she might have a revolution which would become the signal for a general revolution in which both revolutions would complement each other.

This same concept is to be found again in Lenin's writings, coupled with the idea of "permanent revolution" which Marx and Engels had developed in their *Address of the Central Committee to the Communist League* in March

---

[2] Published first as a newspaper article. Reprinted since in various editions of selected works of Marx and Engels.

1850. In that there was placed before the German working class, in the event of a seizure of power by the democratic petty bourgeoisie, the task of carrying the revolution further forward, of declaring the revolution permanent. At the same time it was pointed out that:

> "If the German workers are not able to attain power and achieve their own class interests without going right through a lengthy revolutionary development, they at least know for a certainty this time that the first act of this approaching revolutionary drama will coincide with the direct victory of their own class in France and will be very much accelerated by it."

The socialist revolution, the direct victory of the working class, can only be achieved in an advanced country, but the signal can be given in a less developed country and that will then serve as the first act of a general revolution. What was applied in the middle of the century to Germany was transferred twenty years later to Russia and at the turn of the century formed the basis for a new theoretical generalisation.

Bourgeois-democratic Revolution under Proletarian Leadership

It was in *Two Tactics of Social Democracy in the Democratic Revolution* (July 1905) that Lenin developed the idea of permanent revolution, of the bourgeois-democratic revolution growing into a socialist revolution, or of a bourgeois-democratic revolution in Russia serving as the signal for a socialist revolution in western Europe. What was new was the thesis that in the conditions then prevailing in Russia a bourgeois-democratic revolution could only be carried through to completion under the leadership of the proletariat. The outcome of the impending revolution in Russia would depend upon whether the working-class adopted the role of stooges of the bourgeoisie or leaders of a peoples' revolution. In backward Russia — which, however, already had at its disposal a developed proletariat — the bourgeois revolution was in one sense more advantageous to the proletariat than to the bourgeoisie. In alliance with the peasantry, who, unlike the Russian bourgeoisie, were interested in the radical destruction of feudal institutions and relations, the proletariat would first of all carry through the bourgeois-democratic revolution in the plebeian manner, that is thoroughly, and then use this alliance to establish a revolutionary-democratic dictatorship of proletariat and peasantry; and then next, in league with the semi-proletarian elements in town and country, they would take up the struggle for the socialist revolution:

> "At the head of the whole of the people, and particularly of the peasantry — for complete freedom, for the consistent democratic revolution, for a republic. At the head of all the toilers and the exploited — for socialism."[3]

The bourgeois-democratic revolution now confronting Russia

> "will not be able (without a whole series of intermediate stages of revolutionary development) to affect the foundations of capitalism. At best it may bring about a radical redistribution of the land to the advantage of the peasantry, establish consistent and full democracy including the formation of a republic, eliminate all the oppressive features of Asiatic bondage, not only in rural but also in factory life, lay the foundation for a thorough improvement in the position of the workers and for a rise in their standard of living, and last but not least — carry the flame of revolution into Europe. Such a victory will by no means transform our bourgeois revolution into a socialist revolution; the democratic revolution will not extend beyond the bounds of bourgeois social and economic relationships; nevertheless, the significance of such a victory for the future development of Russia and of the whole world will be immense. Nothing will raise the revolutionary energy of the world proletariat so much, nothing will shorten the path leading to its complete victory to such an extent, as this decisive victory of the revolution that has now started in Russia."[4]

And in an article in which he analysed the tasks and composition of the provisional government which would result from a bourgeois-democratic revolution Lenin repeated that this Russian revolution would start a revolutionary conflagration in Europe; the European worker now languishing under bourgeois reaction would then rise up and show the Russians how to do it; this concerted revolutionary upsurge in Europe would have repercussions in Russia and a period of a few years of revolution would be transformed into an epoch of several revolutionary decades.

[3] Collected Works Vol. 9 p. 114.
[4] *Ibid.* pp. 56—7.

However novel Lenin's concept was, especially with regard to the problem of the Russian revolution, in essentials it still stayed within the framework of Marx's model: the proletariat of the advanced capitalist countries will show the Russian workers the way forward once the Russians have set the whole of Europe ablaze by taking the lead in a bourgeois-democratic revolution. It was the world war, and his researches into imperialism and monopoly capitalism, that led Lenin to work out, step by step, a really new theory of socialist revolution.

In 1914, at the beginning of the war, we find ourselves at first on familiar ground. In *The War and Russian Social Democracy* (November) Lenin is repeating that in Russia the bourgeois-democratic revolution stands on the order of the day and "that in all the advanced countries the war has placed the slogan of socialist revolution on the order of the day."[5] But as early as 1915 Lenin takes things a definite stage further. He starts with the Basle Manifesto of the Second International, which had been disregarded by almost all the social-democratic parties. This had imposed a duty on the working-class movement of using the economic and political crisis arising from the outbreak of war to precipitate the abolition of capitalist class rule. In view of the revolutionary bearing of the Russian proletariat the fulfilment of this task in Russia would come close to a socialist revolution and link up with the general socialist revolution in Europe. "Long live the world-wide brotherhood of the workers and the international revolution of the proletariat!" we read in the manifesto *Concerning the War* (1915); and in the article *The Defeat of Russia and the Revolutionary Crisis* (September 1915) it is clear what he means:

> "The imperialist war has linked up the Russian revolutionary crisis, which stems from a bourgeois-democratic revolution, with the growing crisis of the proletarian socialist revolution in the West. This link is so direct that no separate solution of revolutionary problems is possible in any single country: the bourgeois-democratic revolution in Russia is now not only a prologue to, but an indivisible and integral part of the socialist revolution in the West. The task of the proletariat in 1905 was to carry the bourgeois-democratic revolution in Russia through to the end so as to kindle the proletarian revolution in the West. In 1915 the second part of this task has acquired an urgency that puts it on a level with the first part."[6]

[5] Collected Works Vol. 21 p. 33.
[6] *Ibid.* p. 379.

The bourgeois-democratic revolution in Russia is no longer seen as the first act of a drama which next goes on to the proletarian revolution in the West and then lastly reacts upon Russia and unleashes the socialist revolution there. The action previously spread over several acts is now compressed into the first act.

Several Socialist Revolutions Simultaneously?

The way Lenin wrestled with the new concept of revolution is interesting and characteristic of him. At the same time as he saw in the crisis unleashed by the war the possibility of Russia experiencing a socialist revolution simultaneously with Western Europe, his researches into the nature of imperialism gave him the first inkling that the socialist revolution need not necessarily be victorious in all European countries at one and the same time. As Marx's model of the socialist revolution winning victory in the developed European countries became familiar to the working-class movement so the idea had spread that this victory would take place at more or less the same time in the various countries of Western Europe. It is quite true that a clear discussion of this problem is only to be found in Engels' *The Principles of Communism* which he wrote before the *Communist Manifesto*; but the idea had become an integral part of the growth of the European working-class movement. In *The Principles* it said:

"19. Question: Is it possible for this revolution to take place in a single country, all on its own?

Answer: No. By creating a world market large-scale industry has brought the peoples of the whole world, especially the civilised ones, into such close association with each other that every single nation is affected by what happens to the others. Moreover, in all the civilised countries social development has been evened out so much that in all these countries bourgeoisie and proletariat have become the two decisive classes of society and the struggle between them has become the main battle of our time. Consequently the communist revolution will not be just a national one; it will advance simultaneously in all the civilised countries i.e. in England, America, France and Germany at least. It will develop quicker or slower in these various countries according to whether it is this country or another one which possesses more advanced industry, greater wealth and a more significant range of productive forces. Therefore it will be carried through most slowly and with the greatest difficulty in Germany, quickest and most easily in England. And it will produce a strong reaction in the remaining countries of the world, completely transforming the way they have developed hitherto and enormously speeding it up. It is a universal revolution and therefore it will have a universal setting and scope."[7]

Gradually, tentatively, Lenin gave this idea a thorough overhaul. In his researches into imperialism (more especially in his classic work *Imperialism: the Highest Stage of Capitalism*, 1916) Lenin defined imperialism as monopoly capitalism, as a higher stage of capitalism in which the social character of production and consequently the material prerequisites for the transition to socialism take on a new quality, exhibiting on every side the signs of a period of transition to a higher social order. At the same time the uneven development of different enterprises, trusts and industrial groupings, and between different countries, leads to an intensification of the struggle between monopolies and to a sharpening of the contradictions between the great imperialist powers controlled by the monopolies, to a struggle between the haves and the have-nots among the world powers for the division and redivision of the world, resulting in the appalling convulsions of imperialist wars. Because of all this, imperialism is the eve of the proletarian socialist revolution; but the revolution will not necessarily occur in all the countries of Europe at the same time. In August 1915, in an article entitled *The United States of Europe Slogan*, Lenin wrote that:

"Uneven economic and political development is an absolute law of capitalism. Consequently the victory of socialism is possible first in a few or even in one single capitalist country."[8]

And in *The Military Programme of the Proletarian Revolution* (written, admittedly, after the February revolution of 1917) we read:

"The development of capitalism proceeds extremely unevenly in different countries. It cannot be otherwise under commodity production. That leads to the inescapable conclusion: Socialism cannot be victorious in all countries simultaneously. It will be victorious first in one or several countries, while the others will remain bourgeois or pre-bourgeois for some time."[9]

[7] Marx—Engels *Werke* Vol. IV p. 374 (Berlin 1959). Not available in English.
[8] Collected Works Vol. 21 p. 342.
[9] Collected Works Vol. 23 p. 79.

During the great debate on the epoch-making question of whether it was possible to build socialism in backward Russia these two passages were always being quoted by Stalin. Leaving aside the fact that in these passages Lenin was undoubtedly equating "socialism" with "the socialist revolution", he never, strictly speaking, explained in any detail how exactly the possibility of a socialist revolution in one country is derived from the uneven development of capitalism. All we have is fragments, aphorisms, and tentative suggestions within the framework of the general analysis of imperialism as the eve of socialism. Lenin developed the idea of permanent revolution, of the bourgeois-democratic revolution growing into the socialist revolution, in the special conditions prevailing in Russia and among the Russian peasantry (see his *Letters from Afar* of April 1917).[10] It was a case of one brick being laid on another, the thing growing bit by bit, until eventually Marx's model of revolution took on a new character.

There is an interesting passage in Lenin's article *The Results of the Discussion on Self-Determination* (July 1916) where, in analysing the elements of socialist revolution, he expresses some ideas which point far into the future:

> "To imagine that social revolution is conceivable without revolts by small nations in the colonies and in Europe, without revolutionary outbursts by a section of the petty bourgeoisie with all its prejudices, without a movement of the politically non-conscious proletarian and semi-proletarian masses against oppression by the landowners, the church, and the monarchy, against national oppression, etc: — to imagine all this is to repudiate social revolution. So, one army lines up in one place and says, "We are for socialism", and another somewhere else and says, "We are for imperialism", and that will be a social revolution! . . .
>
> "Whoever expects a 'pure' social revolution will never live to see it. Such a person pays lip-service to revolution without understanding what revolution is . . .
>
> The socialist revolution in Europe cannot be anything other than an outburst of mass struggle on the part of all and sundry oppressed and discontented elements. Inevitably, sections of the petty bourgeoisie and of the backward workers will participate in it — without such

[10] Collected Works Vol. 23 pp. 295—342.

participation, mass struggle is impossible, without it no revolution is possible . . ."[11]

In these reflections Lenin came close to the problems of the October Revolution — and indeed, as I see it, even went beyond it in certain respects.

The New Concept

A coherent defence of the new concept of revolution, as it had been actually experienced in the Russian revolution, is to be found in one of the last of Lenin's works. In *Our Revolution* (January 1923) Lenin set out to demolish the objection (which was being raised in the name of Marxism) that it had been wrong to carry through a socialist revolution in a backward country — that it was contrary to the ideas developed by Marx and Engels. Lenin drew attention to the effects of the imperialist war:

> "Such a revolution was bound to reveal new features or variations resulting from the war itself, for the world has never seen such a war in such a situation."

People say (he went on) that the objective economic prerequisites for socialism are lacking in Russia. And it does not occur to any of the critics to ask:

> "But what about a people that found itself in a revolutionary situation such as that created during the first imperialist war? Might it not, influenced by the hopelessness of its situation, fling itself into a struggle that would offer it at least some chance of securing conditions for the further development of civilisation that were somewhat unusual?"

We ought not, then, to have carried through the revolution because Russia has not yet reached the necessary level of development of the productive forces?

> "But what if the situation, which drew Russia into the imperialist world war that involved every more or less influential West European country and made her a witness of the eve of the revolutions maturing or partly already begun in the East, gave rise to circumstances that

[11] Collected Works, Vol. 22 pp. 355—356.

put Russia and her development in a position which enabled us to achieve precisely that combination of a 'peasant war' with the working-class movement suggested in 1856 by no less a Marxist than Marx himself as a possible prospect for Prussia?"

And, prophetically:

"They are complete strangers to the idea that while the development of world history as a whole follows general laws it is by no means precluded, but, on the contrary, presumed, that certain periods of development may display peculiarities in either the form or the sequence of this development. For instance, it does not even occur to them that because Russia stands on the border-line between the civilised countries and the countries which this war has for the first time definitely brought into the orbit of civilisation — all the Oriental, non-European countries — she could and was, indeed, bound to reveal certain distinguishing features; although these, of course, are in keeping with the general line of world development, they distinguish her revolution from those which took place in the West European countries and introduce certain partial innovations as the revolution moves on to the countries of the East."[12]

Stalin also underlined these peculiarities within the general law of development immediately after Lenin's death in *The Foundations of Leninism* (1924). His sketch of the new Leninist theory of proletarian revolution has become famous in the Communist movement. Imperialism has developed into a single world system, the unevenness of its development leads to wars, and these shatter the whole system; the chain of the system gives way at its weakest link. That, in 1917, was Russia; where will the chain break on the next occasion? Not necessarily where industry is most highly developed, Stalin answered. Perhaps in India, where the proletariat has the national liberation movement as its ally; perhaps in Germany. Imperialism, the whole imperialist system, is just moribund capitalism: thus Stalin in his simplified presentation abandoned Lenin's important idea about the maturing of the material conditions for the transition to socialism under monopoly capitalism — really more because this corresponded to Marx's model than because it was felt to be important for the new concept.

Lenin's disciples have not always fully understood the fundamental novelty of Lenin's concept. Somehow or other the correction of Marx's

[12] Collected Works, Vol. 33 pp. 477, 478.

model got reduced to the notion that the October revolution, although it exhibited distinctive features, did so "in accordance with the general law governing social development". The Sixth World Congress of the Communist International (1928) distinguished between (first) the most highly developed countries, which were confronted by an immediate socialist revolution; then the countries at an intermediate stage of capitalist development which would carry the bourgeois-democratic revolution through to completion and develop it into a socialist revolution; then the colonial, semi-colonial and dependent countries which would have to go through a long period of transitional growth of the bourgeois-democratic revolution into the socialist revolution; and (finally) the completely backward countries where in a similar way nationalist uprisings, the national movement, would smooth the path to socialism if the socialist revolutions of the advanced countries helped them. And the President of the Communist International, Zinoviev, wrote in an article on *The Line of Advance of the Revolution* (March 1926): "Thus we arrive at the order: Europe first, then the East, and finally America."

But to-day it is clear that the failure — the absence — of socialist revolutions in the advanced countries, together with the overthrow of capitalism first in one and subsequently in other backward countries, has modified the general law of revolution in a very far-reaching way. Lenin's suggestion that national revolutions could become a component part of the general revolution and that the special features of the backward countries of the East would affect the general working of the law of revolution has been confirmed over such a wide field that the general law has been altered to a great extent and Marx's 'model' has turned out to be inconsistent with most of the revolutions led by Marxists. Reality has proved to be richer and more colourful than the concept, the revolutions more complicated and varied than the law as compressed in the model, and the general law has worked out much more generally than was originally assumed. Indeed capitalism has been overthrown in a number of countries where it could scarcely be said that the development of the industrial forces of production had already brought them to the brink of the new society. The general law of motion of history has revealed itself as a general tendency whose direction is firmly established but which is realised through human beings, leaving plenty of room for the interaction of subjective and objective factors.

9

SOME MARGINAL NOTES ON A DISCUSSION

Contrary to the assertions made in popular and vulgar accounts of the matter, Lenin did not leave behind any finished theory of revolution. He worked out his theory about the bourgeois-democratic revolution developing into a socialist revolution by considering Russia's special circumstances; then in the conditions of the imperialist war he developed his theory further, on the basis of his researches into monopoly capitalism, the pivot of it being his recognition of the uneven development of capitalism. He also analysed the problem of the allies of the revolutionary proletariat and the significance of the nationalist element in the revolutionary development of the East; and from this he drew far-reaching conclusions about the perspective for world revolution. But these different judgments and ideas and suggestions of Lenin's were only put together after his death, when the great debate flared up about whether it was possible to build socialism in one country, and in such a backward country as Russia. As this was against all the ideas to be found in Marx and Engels every participant in the discussion appealed to Lenin. From the point of view of the problems of theory with which we are concerned in this essay it was a struggle about the adaptation of Marx's model of revolution to the reality of the Russian revolution.

In saying farewell to the workers of Switzerland[1] Lenin wrote on 8th April 1917:

"To the Russian proletariat has fallen the great honour of initiating the series of revolutions which are arising from the imperialist war with objective inevitability. But the idea that the Russian proletariat is a chosen revolutionary proletariat among the workers of the world is absolutely alien to us. We know full well that the proletariat of Russia is less organised, less prepared, less class-conscious than the proletariat of other countries. It is not any particular virtues it possesses,

[1] Lenin, arrested in Austria at the outbreak of war as a Russian spy but released when the authorities realised he was opposed to the Tsar, had then gone to neutral Switzerland. He was enabled to return to Russia after the outbreak of the February revolution. (Trs.)

but rather the specific historical circumstances, that have made the proletariat of Russia for a certain, perhaps very brief, period the vanguard of the world revolutionary proletariat.

Russia is a peasant country, one of the most backward of European countries. Socialism cannot triumph there directly at once. But the peasant character of the country, coupled with the vast landed estates of the noble landlords, may, to judge by the experience of 1905, give tremendous scope to the bourgeois-democratic revolution is Russia, and make our revolution a prelude to and a step towards the world socialist revolution . . .

Such a revolution would not in itself be a socialist revolution. But it would give a great impetus to the world labour movement. It would greatly strengthen the position of the socialist proletariat in Russia and its influence on the agricultural workers and the poor peasants. It would, on the strength of this influence, enable the revolutionary proletariat to develop such organisations as the 'Soviets of Workers' Deputies' to replace the old instruments of oppression of the bourgeois states — the army, the police and the bureaucracy — and under the pressure of the intolerable burden of the imperialist war and its consequences, to carry through a series of revolutionary measures to control the production and distribution of goods.

The Russian proletariat single-handed cannot complete the socialist revolution. But it can lend such a sweep to the Russian revolution as will create the most favourable conditions for a socialist revolution, and, in a sense, start that revolution. It can render more favourable the conditions under which its most important, most trustworthy and most reliable collaborator, the European and American socialist proletariat, embarks upon its own decisive battles . . .

The objective conditions of the imperialist war make it certain that the revolution will not be limited to the first stage of the Russian revolution, that the revolution will not be limited to Russia.

The German proletariat is the most trustworthy and the most reliable ally of the Russian and the world proletarian revolution."[2]

This was the essence of Lenin's standpoint after the February revolution of 1917: he saw the bourgeois-democratic revolution in Russia developing into a socialist revolution and serving as a beacon for a socialist revolution

[2] *Farewell Letter to the Swiss Workers* (8th April 1917). Collected Works Vol. 23 pp. 371—3.

throughout Europe. When the revolution in Western Europe collapsed Lenin shifted the emphasis to the need to carry through the socialist revolution in Russia even if it did not coincide with a socialist revolution in the West. On the fourth anniversary of the October revolution he wrote:

"We have brought the bourgeois-democratic revolution to completion as nobody has done before. We are advancing towards the socialist revolution, consciously, deliberately and undeviatingly, knowing that no Chinese wall separates it from the bourgeois-democratic revolution, and knowing, too, that struggle alone will determine (in the long run) how far we shall advance, what portion of this immeasurably great task we shall accomplish, and to what extent we shall succeed in consolidating our victories. Time will show. But we see even now that a tremendous amount (tremendous for this disorganised, exhausted and backward country) has already been done towards the socialist transformation of society."

And further:

"But in order to render the achievements of the bourgeois-democratic revolution lasting for the peoples of Russia, we were obliged to go further; and we did go further. We solved the problems of the bourgeois-democratic revolution in passing, as a 'by-product' of the main and genuinely proletarian-revolutionary socialist work. We always said that reforms are a by-product of the revolutionary class struggle. We said — and proved by deeds — that bourgeois-democratic reforms are a by-product of proletarian i.e. of the socialist, revolution.

It should be stated that the Kautskys, Hilferdings, Martovs, Chernovs, Hillquits, Longuets, Macdonalds, Turatis, and the other heroes of 'Two-and-a-half' Marxism, were incapable of understanding this relation between the bourgeois-democratic and the socialist revolutions. The first grows into the second. The second, in passing, solves the problems of the first. The second consolidates the work of the first. Struggle, and struggle alone, decides how far the second will succeed in outgrowing the first."[3]

And the first steps in the construction of a socialist economy in town and country were all part of this struggle.

[3] *The Fourth Anniversary of the October Revolution* (14th October 1921). Collected Works, Vol. 33 pp. 51—2, 54.

After Lenin's death, controversy raged among the Russian Communists about whether socialism could be built in such a backward country against the background of the revolutionary tide in western Europe ebbing and capitalism stabilising itself. Those who argued against its being possible to build socialism in Russia were trying to defend Marx's model against the actual situation brought about in Russia by the Marxists. Those who championed the possibility of socialist construction in Russian tried to incorporate this reality into the model, as something peculiarly Russian which still fitted into the framework of the general law.

The traditional approach bred scepticism and doubt, even passivity. Rosa Luxemburg was adopting this approach when she maintained that "the socialist order of society can only be achieved internationally",[4] and so was Otto Bauer when he prophesied that the construction of a socialist society in Russia was a Communist illusion which was bound to be shattered "by the very low level of development of the productive forces".[5]

And Trotsky's attempt to combine his interpretation of Marx's formula about permanent revolution with the October revolution was all part of the same attitude.

Trotsky, Bukharin and Stalin

Trotsky never properly understood Lenin's theory about the bourgeois-democratic revolution in Russia. (His biographer, Isaac Deutscher, did not understand it either). Trotsky's version of the idea of permanent revolution — "Away with the Tsar, bring in government by the workers" — had meant (and this was Lenin's objection to it) skipping over the still uncompleted peasants' movement, failing to appreciate the part the peasantry could play in the revolutionary development of such a backward country as Russia, and losing sight, thanks to the leadership of the bourgeois democratic revolution by the proletariat, of the real content of that revolution. Events pushed this controversy into the background: the rapid transition of the bourgeois-democratic revolution into a socialist revolution allowed it to be forgotten. But in the great debate about the possibility of

[4] Rosa Luxemburg: *Die Russische Revolution*, p. 119.
[5] Otto Bauer, *Der neue Kurs in Sowjetrussland* (Vienna, 1921) p. 31. Otto Bauer was one of the leaders of the Austrian Social-Democratic Party, and adopted a friendly attitude to the Russian revolution.

building socialism in Russia, and in the absence of a revolution in the West, it once more assumed importance.

Trotsky seized on the idea of permanent revolution and attempted, in the name of the traditional Marxist ideas, to fight against the swing towards the construction of socialism in Russia, against its construction in one single country. In such a backward peasant country, he declared, the revolution was bound to lead to serious conflicts between the proletariat and the broad masses of the peasantry, and these conflicts could only be resolved on an international scale in the arena of the world-wide proletarian revolution. Without state support from the European proletariat, revolutionary Russia would not be able to keep going for long in a conservative Europe, and only after the victory of the proletariat in the chief European countries could they really begin to build a truly socialist economy in Russia. Trotsky defended the classic concept of the revolution and at the same time put a Bonapartist edge on it by saying that it was necessary to carry the revolution into other countries, so as to save the Russian revolution by means of revolution in the advanced countries. Gramsci talked about a combination of "vecchio meccanismo" (the old 'mechanicalism') with "napoleonismo anacronistico" (an anachronistic 'Napoleonism').

Bukharin's answer furnished a whole row of arguments (and quotations from Lenin) which Stalin was to make use of when assuming the lead in the discussion and when winding it up. Bukharin reproached Trotsky for never having understood the special features of the Russian revolution, for never having freed himself from 'Europeanism', and for not seeing that the question of winning over the peasants as allies in the bourgeois-democratic revolution, and in the development of the bourgeois-democratic revolution into a socialist revolution, had a tremendous international significance for future revolutions. Trotsky (Bukharin said) just stuck to the general rules and failed to see the special features.

Stalin, in answering Trotsky and Zinoviev, summed up the elements of the Leninist theory of revolution in an understandable though simplified form. He preached the gospel of the possibility of socialism in one country (in the true spirit of Lenin's ideas, as it seems to me) and he opposed Trotsky's "intelletualismo massimalistico" (his extreme intellectualism)[6] in a realistic and down-to-earth way. The revolution in Western Europe

[6] Giulano Procacci, *La rivoluzione permanente e il socialismo in un paese solo* (1963) p. 92.

had simply not materialised; what kind of social order then, should the victorious proletariat establish?

In this epoch-making discussion one problem came up whose significance extends beyond the special case of the Russian revolution. Lenin had already seized on it when speaking about the peculiar features of the Russian revolution. He spoke about the effects of the imperialist war on revolutionary developments in Russia, about the possibility of the victorious revolution taking advantage of imperialist rivalries among the capitalist powers and being able, thanks to the vast extent of its territory, to hold on to power despite the attacks of imperialist intervention; and about the existence of a deep-seated revolutionary movement among the peasants, whose demands could be taken up and satisfied by the revolutionary proletariat. But, (he went on), "these specific conditions do not exist in Western Europe at present; and a repetition of such or similar conditions will not come about easily. That is why, apart from a number of other causes, it will be more difficult to start a socialist revolution in Western Europe than it was for us."[7]

[7] *"Left-Wing" Communism: An Infantile Disorder* (1920) (Chap. VII.) Collected Works, Vol. 31, p. 64.

10

SKIPPING SOME STAGES OF THE REVOLUTION

Lenin's greatness as a theoretician consists in the fact that he supplemented and replaced Marx's model of the socialist revolution with a new model which was then borne out by the October revolution. The decisive factor in what might be called this truly Copernican change was his analysis of monopoly capitalism, of imperialism, and of the special features of the revolutionary perspective in Russia, particularly the problem of how the bourgeois-democratic revolution could grow into a socialist revolution. However, looking at it from the point of view of basic philosophical principles, an equally decisive factor was Lenin's stand against the emasculation of Marx's law of motion of society, against its reduction to a kind of fatalism, and the special consideration which he gave to the subjective factor, to decisions of the human will. This had been conspicuous already in *What is to be Done?* Lenin never allowed himself to separate the question of what is going to happen from the question of what is to be done.

Another significant thing in this regard is the attention which Lenin gave to the revolutionary nationalist movements of the East (in marked contrast to the 'general laws' and habits of thought and orientation of the Second International). A little essay of his called *Backward Europe and Advanced Asia* (May 1913) has become famous.

In this article Lenin said that while increasingly the European bourgeoisie was only capable of beastliness and brutality, in China the bourgeois elements were drawing closer to the people in the fight against reaction:

"A hundred million people are awakening to life and light and freedom. What joy this great world movement brings to the hearts of all class-conscious workers who understand that the way to collectivism leads through democracy! What keen sympathy all true democrats feel for the young Asia!"[1]

Even more significant and fundamental is the pointer given in *A Caricature of Marxism* (1916) where Lenin emphasises the importance of the

[1] Collected Works Vol. 19 p. 101.

84

national liberation movement in the East for the whole perspective of revolution in the world:

"The social revolution cannot come about except in the form of an epoch of proletarian civil war against the bourgeoisie in the advanced countries combined with a whole series of democratic and revolutionary movements, including movements for national liberation, in the undeveloped, backward and oppressed nations."[2]

After the October revolution, which confirmed his new concept of revolution, Lenin put the emphasis on that part of the concept which had a bearing on the national revolutionary anti-imperialist movements of the East, and on the recognition of these movements as an integral part of the world revolution. At the Third World Congress of the Communist International, in July 1921, Lenin said:

"It is perfectly clear that in the impending battles in the world revolution, the movement of the majority of the population of the globe, initially directed towards national liberation, will turn against capitalism and imperialism and will, perhaps, play a much more revolutionary part than we expect. It is important to emphasise the fact that, for the first time in our International, we have taken up the question of preparing for this struggle. Of course, there are many more difficulties in this enormous sphere than in any other, but at all events the movement is advancing. And in spite of the fact that the masses of toilers — the peasants in the colonial countries — are still backward, they will play a very important revolutionary part in the coming phases of the world revolution."[3]

The October Revolution was the beginning of the world revolution, of a process which, starting with the transfer of the capitalist means of production to social ownership in one country, would conclude with the victory of socialism in all countries. Just as the creation of the imperialist system had meant that an assessment of a particular country's chances of revolution must no longer be based simply on factors inside that country, but must also take into account the international position of the country in question, so equally the beginning of the world revolution meant that the

[2] Collected Works Vol. 23 p. 60.
[3] *Report on the Tactics of the Russian Communist Party;* Lenin, Collected Works, Vol. 32 p. 482.

revolutionary perspectives of this or that country had to be assessed in the context of the fact that the world revolution had already begun. That was why Lenin was able to say about countries which were economically more backward than Tsarist Russia and were suffering from colonial oppression as well:

> "Meanwhile, India and China are seething. They represent over 700 million people, and together with the neighbouring Asian countries, that are in all ways similar to them, over half of the world's inhabitants. Inexorably and with mounting momentum they are approaching their 1905, with the essential and important difference that in 1905 the revolution in Russia could still proceed (at any rate at the beginning) in isolation, that is, without other countries being immediately drawn in. But the revolutions that are maturing in India and China are being drawn into — have already been drawn into — the revolutionary struggle, the revolutionary movement, the world revolution."[4]

And Lenin became even clearer, visionary really, about the revolutionary development of the backward colonial countries when he wrote in his last work, on 2nd March 1923:

> "In the last analysis, the outcome of the struggle will be determined by the fact that Russia, India, China, etc., account for the overwhelming majority of the population of the globe. And during the past few years it is this majority that has been drawn into the struggle for emancipation with extraordinary rapidity, so that there cannot be the slightest doubt what the final outcome of the struggle will be. In this sense, the complete victory of socialism is fully and absolutely assured."[5]

Lenin's optimism was also based on the conviction that in several of the backward countries of the East the storm of national anti-colonial revolutions would take on a socialist direction, that new forms of transition to socialism would arise and that — as he said in July 1920 at the Second Congress of the Communist International — it was wrong to "assume that the capitalist phase of development is inevitable in the backward countries".

---

[4] *On the Tenth Anniversary of Pravda* (1922); Collected Works, Vol. 33 p. 350.
[5] *Better Fewer, but Better* (1923); *ibid* p. 500.

The fact that this pointer of Lenin's has not won the fame which it deserves is due, not least, to the fact that the vulgarisation of Marxism has resulted in a wide-spread notion that hitherto different social formations have always succeeded one another in a straight line: that primitive society has always been followed by slavery, and slavery by feudalism. This over-simplified picture of the law of motion of society is to be found not only in the writings of Lenin's opponents (who use it as a political argument) but in the historical narratives of Lenin's disciples, too.

It does not correspond either to the historical facts or to the views of Marx who, for example, in his work *Pre-Capitalist Economic Formations* (1857—58) described how amongst the Germanic peoples the transition from tribal society to feudalism took place without any intermediate stage of slavery, at a time when slavery was already crumbling.

After the Second World War

Lenin had spoken about the effects of the First World War on the per-spectives and development of the Russian revolution and about the special features which resulted from it. For a number of countries the effects of the Second World War on their revolutionary prospects were even more far-reaching, because the land of the October Revolution was a belligerent power and emerged from the war as a great victorious power. For some countries certain special features of the October Revolution necessarily became still more "special", and in the countries of the East (as Lenin had already foreseen) they proved to have a very great potency indeed. For several countries it could not be a matter of indifference how far the Soviet Union and her army would be able to influence the country's devel-opment, whether the country was going to find itself in the geographical vicinity of the Soviet Union and occupied by the Soviet Army. In his presentation of Leninism Stalin had talked about the imperialist system snapping at its weakest link, and how this did not necessarily have to be a country whose industry was highly developed. And in fact the chain only did break in countries which, almost all, had only experienced a slight industrial development and which *above all* were almost all close to the place where the chain had been broken on the first occasion. All the coun-tries where, after the Second World War, capitalist private property in the means of production was abolished were, with the exception of Czecho-slovakia, the backward countries of Eastern Europe and Asia. In all these countries the national liberation struggle played an important part to such an extent in the colonial countries that one is obliged in referring to these countries to speak of a new model of socialist revolution.

Stalin used to maintain — and in a number of Communist writings one can still find the same assertion to-day — that the victory of the Soviet Union in the Second World War was "inevitable". But this is by no means the case. A mode of life which constitutes a higher level of social development does not necessarily win wars, as is shown by the defeat of the French under Napoleon at the hands of Tsarist Russia. But equally it was not in the least "inevitable" (as a number of critics of Marxism argue) that after the October Revolution the abolition of the capitalist ownership of the means of production should once more occur (with the exception of Czechoslovakia) only in backward, mainly agricultural, countries. It was partly due to the fact that the countries in question were neighbours of the Soviet Union and so, thanks to the course taken by the second world war, were occupied by the Soviet Army. The only "inevitable" thing about these revolutions was that it was possible to make use of the incompleteness of the bourgeois-democratic revolution: agrarian revolutions took place which abolished the remnants of feudalism and feudal institutions. Furthermore, the anti-fascist liberation struggle against alien fascist rule — and the anti-colonial independence struggle against imperialist oppression — lent a national-revolutionary momentum to the development of things. And it was in the nature of things that the general tendency of the law of motion should have asserted its influence upon the direction of social development.

The fact that, in a number of countries, this revolution was made far easier by the military assistance of the Soviet troops is irrelevant to the problem we are here concerned with. It was certainly of great importance for these countries' own practical problems, and for problems of theory in the international working-class movement. But it is less important in relation to the theme that occupies us here, namely, the assessment of which features of the socialist revolution are decisive for the abolition of private capitalist ownership in the means of production. History knows of no new mode of production becoming internationally prevalent without foreign influences having been decisive in some country or other, in this or that zone. Otherwise people would never have got beyond the Stone Age in regions where no metals occurred. On the other hand, there were and are quite a number of countries in which the old form of society has only been preserved and kept going for a while longer by means of foreign influences. Besides, it is all too often ignored that in Czechoslovakia and in Bulgaria powerful Communist Parties existed; and the victory of the Yugoslav partisans, though supported certainly by the military operations and offensives of the Soviet army, was largely the result of their own strength. What is decisive, however, in relation to the problems we are discussing here is that throughout history the general diffusion of a new form of society has never yet occurred without its victory in one or more countries having reacted on other countries in some form or other.

The country which had been the first to overthrow the capitalist ownership of the means of production was bound to have some effect on the development of those countries where there was a possibility of abolishing the capitalist ownership of the means of production. It was bound to be very telling when the land of the October Revolution emerged from the Second World War as a mighty victor. And it did in fact result in the general law of motion of society being realised in these countries in a whole series of new ways which were distinctive and special to the countries in question.

The Example of the Chinese Revolution

It was of the essence of the new revolutions that they occurred in backward countries (Czechoslovakia excepted), and the impetus of the national liberation struggle was crucial for the transition from a bourgeois-democratic revolution to a socialist revolution. In the revolutions in Asia this nationalist impulse, which Lenin had already detected, attained a new quality, especially in China and Vietnam, where, in contradistinction to Korea, the revolutions — although undoubtedly affected by the victory of the Soviet Union and the prestige from it — were carried through without the presence of Soviet troops.

The theory and practice of the Chinese Revolution, which occurred in a country far more backward than Tsarist Russia and one dominated and attacked by foreign imperialism, has a more than local importance. In the Chinese Revolution we have a problem that cannot be understood simply in terms of Lenin's concept. It is no accident that from the very beginning "the Chinese question" led to heated discussions inside the working-class movement. And there is a residue from these discussions which has never been disposed of.

Trotsky, who had never entirely grasped Lenin's concept of revolution, tried to force the Chinese revolution, too, into the mould of Marx's model — as interpreted by himself. The slogan and solution advanced by him was an immediate proletarian revolution, irreconcilable struggle against the national bourgeoisie, and the dictatorship of the proletariat. Stalin took his stand on Lenin's concept as it had been realised in Russia. His slogan was the democratic dictatorship of the proletariat and peasantry, (branded as a betrayal of the revolution by Trotsky), and he tried to incorporate various peculiarities of the Chinese situation into Lenin's idea of the bourgeois-democratic revolution developing into a socialist revolution. While Trotsky's and Stalin's supporters were arguing the toss like this, Mao Tse-tung worked out a model that *did* apply to China: a country incomparably more backward than Tsarist Russia with a much less developed proletariat, where the peasant question was bound to be the main issue of the revolution; a country, too, exploited and controlled by foreign imperialism in which revolutionary nationalist impulses necessarily assumed a decisive significance. Let us trace the development of this new model.

In March 1926 Mao Tse-tung published an article entitled *An Analysis of the Classes in Chinese Society*. In it he pointed out that the modern industrial proletariat in China numbered only two millions. All the same, "the industrial proletariat is the leading force in our revolution" said he, like a good boy.[6] But the article in fact gave twice as much attention to the peasantry as to "the leading force".

In March 1927 came his *Report of an Investigation into the Peasant Movement in Hunan*. And the basic idea which he derived from his researches was that the main force in the Chinese Revolution would be the poor peasantry, comprising 70 per cent of the village population, and that the main content of the Chinese Revolution would be the agrarian revolution:

"In a very short time, in China's central, southern and northern provinces, several hundred million peasants will rise like a tornado or tempest, a force so extraordinarily swift and violent that no power, however great, will be able to suppress it. . . . the peasant eye does not err."[7]

[6] *Selected Works of Mao Tse-tung*, Vol. I p. 20 (English ed. 1954)
[7] *Ibid.* pp. 21—22.

In September 1928 he wrote *The Character of the Revolution*, defending the line of the Chinese Communists against the Trotskyists, defending their view that it was an essential preliminary to the transition to socialism to carry through the bourgeois-democratic revolution first, which would consist principally in an agrarian revolution and in the abolition of feudal relationships. But from the way the "red districts" (situated almost exclusively in the villages) actually operated it is apparent that in practice Mao Tse-tung modified Lenin's concept, not only as regards Trotskyist formulas for permanent revolution, but also in respect of Stalin's spokesmen and the ideas they were propounding in the Communist International, which clung too closely to the Russian concept. The years 1930 to 1934 bear witness to the struggles going on inside the party when Li Li-san and Wan Min, with the support of Stalin and the Communist International, attacked the "peasant narrowness" and the "conservatism" of "village strategists" and when the official line aimed at developing proletarian uprisings in the big cities — because, after all, the proletariat is the leading force in the bourgeois-democratic revolution, is it not? They asserted that the main thing was to prepare for socialist revolution, and pressed for the extension of the armed struggle to the big cities and for a struggle against the "middle sections"; and they contrasted this with "peasant revolutionariness" which stood in the way of the "bolshevisation" of the party. In reply Mao Tse-tung claimed to be acting in accordance with the Leninist concept, which actually no longer covered all the developments in the Chinese situation.

The struggle against Japanese imperialism underlined the nationalist antiimperialist character of the Chinese Revolution, but at the same time, and for that very reason, pointed to the agrarian revolution as the revolution's main content and the way forward to a socialist revolution. In Mao Tsetung's article *On the Tactics of Fighting Japanese Imperialism* (December 1935) we read that "the Chinese revolution at the present stage is still a bourgeois-democratic revolution not a proletarian-socialist one, as counterrevolutionary Trotskyists" assert, and that because of China's backwardness the transition to a socialist revolution "is much more difficult and requires a good deal more time and effort for China than for Russia".[8]

In his work *Questions of Strategy in China's Revolutionary War* (December 1936) China's armed struggle is characterised as "a revolutionary agrarian

---

[8] *Ibid.* pp. 172—3.

war" in both form and content, in which the proletariat and the Chinese Communist Party are taking the lead. Here certainly his terminology still contains a residue of the Russian concept which did not correspond to the realities of the Chinese situation. The revolution was based on the "red districts", or after the Long March on the "special districts", and during the anti-Japanese war on the peasant masses who were led by the Communist Party; and the leadership of the party consisted throughout of Marxist intellectuals. Mao Tse-tung's formulations about this ignore the basic facts, under the spell of the traditional formulas, and perhaps also with an eye to the contest with the standard-bearers of the old 'model'. The article talks about the peasantry being led by the proletariat and the Communist Party, and in the same breath describes how in the revolutionary agrarian war it is the mass of the peasantry and urban petty-bourgeoisie who constitute the main force in that revolutionary war. And the main content of the revolutionary war is the agrarian revolution which is being carried through under the leadership of China's Communist Party.

In *The Tasks of the Chinese Communist Party* (May 1937) he talks about the leadership of the proletariat in the anti-Japanese war, which really only makes sense on the assumption that the Chinese Communist Party was the vanguard of the proletariat. But in the studies devoted to the military problems of the anti-Japanese war *(The Protracted War, The Place of the Communist Party of China in the National War, The War and Questions of Strategy)*, what is stressed again and again is that the struggle is based on the village, that the main question is the peasant question and that the towns will only be captured from the villages. What will secure victory is not some scheme for a proletarian uprising in the towns but the strongpoints in the villages, the bases in the countryside, and the partisan warfare of the peasants. "The armed struggle of the Communist Party of China is a peasant war under the leadership of the proletariat" a proletariat whose revolutionary élite numbering 450,000 had been slaughtered by Chiang Kai-shek back in 1927—29.

The inconsistencies in a number of formulations such as these were simply due to the fact that the special problems of the Chinese revolution could not be adequately dealt with in terms of Marx's and Lenin's concepts and ideas about revolution. This comes out even more clearly in Mao Tse-tung's work *The Chinese Revolution and the Chinese Communist Party* (December 1939). He analysed the separate classes of Chinese society in relation to the task of "throwing off the yoke of foreign imperialism . . . throwing off the yoke of feudal relations in the ownership of the land". The agrarian revolution needs to be conducted as a national revolution and the national revolution as an agrarian revolution. The national bourgeoisie is split and only "relatively reliable". The peasants, constituting 80 per cent of the population, provide the bulk of the revolution. The proletariat number $2\frac{1}{2}$ to 3 million in industry and 12 million wage-earners in small-scale industry and trade. They are the most revolutionary class; there are very few blacklegs among them, and no reformist political party; they are "the mainspring of the Chinese revolution", "the most class-conscious of all the classes in Chinese society". Mao never explains how this squares with the fact that the proletariat was largely recruited from ruined peasantry. The agrarian revolution is all of a piece with the national revolution. The great importance of the battle against Japanese imperialism lies in the fact that it is a national revolution against imperialism; it is "the democratic revolution" which — thanks to the existence of the Soviet Union and to the fact that the Chinese revolution is being led by the Chinese Communist Party — is already "part of the proletarian world revolution". The "anti-imperialist, anti-feudal revolution of the broad masses of the people under the leadership of the proletariat" sets the stage for the socialist revolution, because it is the socialist revolution, led by the party of the Chinese proletariat (the Chinese Communist Party), which will complete the tasks of the bourgeois-democratic revolution.

On New Democracy (January 1940) is the basic work in which Mao Tse-tung gives us his most mature exposition of the new model, though he had worked it all out some time before that. The article is based on the idea that "the struggle of the peasantry for land and soil constitutes the main content of the anti-imperialist and anti-feudal struggle in China, that the bourgeois-democratic revolution in China is basically a peasant revolution". In the course of the national revolutionary struggle against imperialism in general, and against Japanese imperialism in particular, the revolution will grow into a new-democratic revolution which, under the leadership of the Communists, will establish the dictatorship of the alliance of all revolutionary classes — a flexible formula suited to China, in place of Lenin's "democratic dictatorship of the workers and peasants", because the national bourgeoisie is expressly indicated as being an ally in the national revolution. Even if the society created by the new democracy is not yet a socialist society, still the new democratic revolution is already a part of the world socialist revolution.

This new concept has a new quality about it because the revolution is a national revolution, because it draws its main strength from the peasantry, and because it is taking place at a point in time when the world revolution has already begun:

> "In an era when the world capitalist front has collapsed in one corner of the globe (a corner which forms one-sixth of the world) ... in such an era, any revolution that takes place in a colony or semi-colony against imperialism, i.e. against the international bourgeoisie and international capitalism, belongs no longer to the old category of bourgeois-democratic world revolution, but to a new category, and is .... part of the new world revolution, the proletarian-socialist world revolution."[9]

National Anti-imperialist Revolution and a Socialist Orientation

This diagnosis may be accepted as a broad outline of the course taken by the national anti-imperialist revolutions which have followed the Chinese Revolution — provided that one fills in the gap in the theoretical explanation about the Chinese situation which is to be found (it seems to me) even in the works of MaoTse-tung. This revolution was one whose chief forces were the peasants: in the battles of the October Revolution the cadres came from the Putilov factory in St. Petersburg; in the battles of the Chinese revolution they came from the villages of Hunan, Kiangsi and Yenan. Second, this revolution was led by Marxist intellectuals. Various conventional formulas are used to conceal this fact, but it cannot be properly accounted for simply by pointing out that the intellectuals of the colonial and semi-colonial countries are not comparable with those of the capitalist countries (as in *Draw in Large Number of Intellectuals*, December, 1939).

The anti-feudal, anti-imperialist revolutions which have a socialist perspective have gone beyond Lenin's model and are creating a new type of socialist revolution in which "the leading role of the proletariat" finds its chief expression in the leading role of intellectuals who have espoused Marxism, the science of the revolutionary proletariat.

Nor is that all. In Cuba the victors of the Sierra Maestra, the revolutionary intellectuals who commanded the peasant contingents in the battle against the Batista dictatorship and American domination, only came to embrace Marxism gradually, after their victory. In Algeria it was two years after

[9] *Selected Works*, Vol. 3, p. 111.

the liberation before the military leadership decided on a programme which combined elements of a Marxist mode of thought with the profession of Islam; and the Algerian constitution, in enumerating the revolutionary classes, declares the correct order of precedence to be: fellaheen, workers, intelligentsia. The reserves of the anti-feudal, anti-imperialist revolution in the colonial and semi-colonial countries have given rise to a new law of motion of socialist revolution which cannot be fitted into either Marx's or Lenin's models, or even into the ideas and theories of the Chinese Revolution. These revolutions confront us with the problem of how to assess the socialist orientation of countries which have an extremely weak proletariat and no developed industry, but which have at their head either a united national revolutionary party which makes use of Marxist ideas and concepts (as in Ghana under Kwame Nkrumah, Guinea and Mali) or an officer class (as in Burma and Egypt — linked in that case with technicians) which nationalises the big banks, large-scale enterprises and foreign capital and adopts a policy of industrialisation under public control. Can such an orientation be designated as anything other than socialist?

For the peoples of Asia, Africa and Latin America socialism is a magic word which has frequently been misused by reactionary cliques. All the same, it seems to me that where industry, the big banks and big business have been nationalised, and the influence of foreign capital in production and business has been eliminated, one can only speak of a socialist orientation, of a novel and complex development which is an integral part of the world socialist revolution. Socialism is more than that, to be sure; but then that applies to other countries as well. But if one grants that the essence of the socialist revolution is the socialisation of the most decisive means of production then one is confronted in the dependent, colonial and semi-colonial countries with the fact that the law of motion of society is being realised in new forms — forms in which the national-revolutionary anti-imperialist revolution (sometimes without expressly anti-feudal features even, because it is concerned in part with pre-feudal relationships) is the prelude, albeit a very long prelude, to the socialist revolution. All this stands in such sharp contrast to people's preconceptions about proletarian socialist revolution that Marxist writers hesitate about the propriety of the term "socialism" and get out of it by using expressions like "anti-capitalist revolution" and "non-capitalist development". But every serious argument involving this sort of expedient would also entail denying the designation "socialist" to the countries to which most of these writers themselves belong. Really it is a matter of measures and tendencies and perspectives which *are* socialist even though it is not possible to say that they have been bound up, from the very start, with leadership by the proletariat.

This problem crops up in the second "Havana Manifesto" (4th February 1962), dealing with the prospects of the revolution in the Latin American countries. The emphasis is put on the national-revolutionary and anti-American character of the prospective revolution, an anti-imperialist and anti-feudal revolution involving the workers, the peasantry, students, intellectuals and the progressive sections of the national bourgeoisie. To quote the actual words:

> "While in the underdeveloped countries of Latin America the working class as a rule is not strong, there does exist one social class which, thanks to the inhuman conditions in which it lives, is potentially a great force. If it is led by the working class and the revolutionary intelligentsia it is capable of playing the decisive role in the struggle for national liberation. This class is the peasantry, for 70 per cent of the total population lives under feudal relationships."

The characterisation of the leading forces of the revolution here is a shade different from Mao Tse-tung's formulations, interestingly: here the revolutionary intelligentsia is expressly named alongside the working class as a leading force. Yet the Latin American countries are, without doubt, the most advanced of the underdeveloped countries: they have a working-class movement with established traditions and some considerable centres of industry — which in many Asian and African countries is not the case.

An Anti-colonial Manifesto

It was the problems of these countries that gave rise to Franz Fanon's book *Les Damnés de la Terre* (The Wretched of the Earth).[10] This anti-colonial manifesto is full of inconsistencies (which are in part a reflection of the novel contradictions of the colonial revolution) and it also contains

[10] 1961. English translation by Constance Farrington, with preface by Sartre, published 1965 (Penguin Books, 1967).

Born in Martinique in 1925, Fanon studied medicine in France and was sent to a hospital in Algeria. His experiences there during the Algerian war of independence convinced him of the justice of the Algerians' cause, and he added the labours of journalist and propagandist to his medical work. The strain broke his health and he died in 1961, aged 36. (Trs.)

a number of incorrect conclusions, which are largely due to Fanon generalising from the experiences and results of the Algerian revolution and applying it to all colonial peoples. But the book is a significant one all the same, not only because he is dealing with the wretched of this earth who even today are still condemned to perpetual hunger, but because his book elucidates the problems of the revolution in the colonial and semi-colonial countries — the problems of the transition from national, anti-imperialist revolutions to the socialist revolution and (consequently) the problems of the perspective of the world socialist revolution.

In the colonies (Fanon writes) and in the national liberation struggle of the oppressed countries two worlds stand face to face, clearly differentiated one from another: the colonisers and the colonised. The foreign domination is complete, so the liberation struggle must be equally thorough: in the Day of Judgment the last shall be first.

When the revolutionary liberation struggle breaks out certain groups try to avoid a violent conflict and try to work out compromises with the colonial rulers on questions of the franchise and economic aid, surrendering national independence in exchange for a measure of self-government. It is the urban political parties and the trade unions, the business, professional and working-class organisations who do this — all of whom Fanon lumps together as being privileged groups under the colonial system. But what these groups forget is that the national liberation struggle is a struggle for human dignity and for their native soil. These nationalist reformist groups cannot satisfy the fundamental needs of the broad masses of the peasantry, "who are not interested in the colonist's legal rights and status but in his property, his farm". It is these dispossessed peasant masses, Fanon indicates, who are the really revolutionary force in the struggle for national liberation. "They have nothing to lose and everything to gain. The peasant, degraded and starving, is the first of the exploited to discover that only violence pays." They constitute the only revolutionary class.

Fanon gives a detailed analysis of his interpretation of the class forces involved in the colonial revolution. The compromising nationalist parties are urban parties, organisations representing the privileged sections, businessmen, officials, professional people and workers, whom Fanon regards as the most privileged sections of the indigenous population. The broad masses of the oppressed peasantry view such parties, and the trade unions, with suspicion because the townsfolk dress like Europeans, they talk the same language as the oppressors and they try to form connections with the colonists. Only the 'lumpenproletariat' on the border between town and country (and all too often a reservoir for the colonial police) belong from the very start to the ranks of the national revolution, ennobling themselves by bloody struggle.

Spontaneous uprisings of the peasantry — such as occurred in Madagascar in 1947 — show us where the power behind the national revolutions in the colonial countries really lies. It is an intellectual élite who show the peasants how to organise, and do the organising. These key men are well aware of the need for occasional compromise but they do not compromise themselves because they have from the first adopted the position that every compromise is only a temporary concession, and that since all the justice is on their side it is only to their side that the concessions are really being made.

Fanon characterises the national bourgeoisie of the colonial countries as an immature bourgeoisie with no historical function to perform: it is the job of the national revolution to put this national bourgeoisie out of existence, to obstruct its development and to bar the way to power for this unnecessary and useless class. It is not necessary for the revolution to have a bourgeois phase in which it is led by the national bourgeoisie. The alliance between the revolutionary intellectuals and the peasant masses makes it possible to nationalise trade by means of co-operative buying and selling organisations, so depriving the parasites of the opportunity of enriching themselves. Wherever possible the leadership of the national revolution should abandon the capital and spread into the countryside and mix amongst the peasantry. That will bring them into direct contact with the peasant masses and enable them to raise the national consciousness of the people to socialism.

In summing up the various experiences of the Algerian revolution Fanon appears to have underestimated the role of the Algerian workers, of the dockers, miners and lorry drivers. The fact that he regards it as impossible to win over sections of the national bourgeoisie in support of the national revolution and even, after the liberation, for the turn towards socialism seems to me to be due to his generalising on the basis of certain peculiarities in the Algerian situation where agriculture, industry and trade were largely dominated by the French settlers. Above all, he overlooks the fact that even the most heroic peasant masses cannot do without the organising ability and education of the working class, whose numbers can only be increased by industrialisation. Moreover, the peasant masses do not constitute one homogeneous class, and they are much more liable than the workers to fall prey to reactionary ideologies, racialist feelings and dangerous fluctuations of mood and temper. A policy directed towards eliminating backwardness and industrialising the country necessarily involves support for the growth and strengthening and increasing importance of the working class, which is readier than other classes to shake off reactionary views and prejudices and which is not intent upon exploiting other sections of the populace.

Nevertheless, it is no good ignoring the fact, brought out very clearly in Fanon's anti-colonial manifesto, that the transformation of the national, anti-imperialist revolutions into socialist revolutions raises a host of new questions, whose complexity has not yet been fully appreciated and which still require a lot of theoretical analysis and discussion. For example, in his book *Partisans against the Generals*, the Australian journalist Wilfrid Burchett, dealing with the class composition of the South Vietnamese Liberation Front, quotes the observation of their military leader that: "It is the peasants who stand in the front line while the workers and intellectuals in the towns, and some of the bourgeoisie, give them support."

Lenin had already pointed out that the colonial revolutions were essentially peasant revolutions. In a report to the second All-Russian Congress of Communist Organizations of the Peoples of the East (November, 1919), he declared:

> "In this respect you are confronted with a task which has not previously confronted the Communists of the world: relying on the general theory and practice of communism, you must adapt yourselves to specific conditions such as do not exist in the European countries; you must be able to apply that theory and practice to conditions in which the bulk of the population are peasants, and in which the task is to wage a struggle against medieval survivals and not against capitalism."[11]

The revolution in the backward countries did not correspond to the conceptions of Marx and Engels; the more backward these countries were, the greater the divergence. And the political structures established in these countries after their revolutions are equally remote from Marx' and Engels' picture of things; and again, the more backward these countries are, the truer it is. Reality, then, has not stuck to the ideas put forward in the classics; but we have got to stick to reality.

Mention has already been made of Lenin's significant comments that these colonial peasant revolutions are taking place at a time when the world

[11] Collected Works Vol. 30 p. 161.

revolution has already begun and that consequently they have been caught up in the current of world revolution. But the transition of these national anti-imperialist revolutions towards socialist revolution has given the problem new dimensions; in their national revolutionary struggle the backward agrarian countries have erected giant ladders which point upwards to the socialist revolution. Fanon's conclusions are wrong, but the facts on which he bases them are true facts. New models of development towards socialism have emerged which have gone beyond Marx's and even Lenin's conceptions and which also cannot be fitted comfortably into theoretical generalisations based on the Chinese Revolution. And the fundamental reason for this, surely, is that other socialist revolutions have already taken place, that the world socialist revolution has begun and is striding forward. The first socialist revolution was bound to give rise to the possibility of other socialist revolutions occurring according to new laws of social development; and the more recent socialist revolutions, in turn, to other new patterns.

In Praise of Backwardness?

Let us recall once more the classic formulation of Marx's model as given in the preface to The Critique of Political Economy:

"At a certain stage of their development, the material productive forces of society come into conflict with the existing relations of production, or — what is but a legal expression for the same thing — with the property relations within which they have been at work hitherto. From forms of development of the productive forces these relations turn into their fetters. Then begins an epoch of social revolution ... No social order ever perishes before all the productive forces for which there is room in it have developed; and new, higher relations of production never appear before the material conditions of their existence have matured in the womb of the old society itself."

It is obvious that the October Revolution had already burst the bounds of this classic model. So it reads oddly when professedly Marxist books claim on the one hand that Lenin replaced Marx's theory of revolution with a new theory, which foresaw the possibility of a revolution occurring in a backward country, and at the same time still spell out Marx's law of motion, illustrating it with this famous quotation from the preface to The Critique of Political Economy, as if that was all there was to be said on the matter. But the October Revolution rapidly destroyed not only feudal property relations but also capitalist property relations, which had, however, in no sense become fetters upon the productive forces developing within them; these relations came to an end at a stage when the productive forces had not yet been developed as far as they might have been within the capitalist relations of production. And this is true to a much greater extent of the anti-feudal, anti-imperialist revolutions in Asia and Africa. There it is in part pre-feudal relationships which have been overthrown; and for them it is even truer than it is for the land of the October Revolution that they have to organise, under more advanced relations of production, the kind of industrialisation and development of the productive forces which took place spontaneously in the advanced capitalist countries. In these countries the productive forces are not the basis for those relations of production which are (looking at things schematically) "next in the queue". Rather, certain stages of development get passed over. This is because there are revolutionary alliances bent upon creating socialist relations of production, which seem to them to be the only suitable ones for the development (the creation, often) of modern productive forces, and also because those sections and classes which might have been responsible for promoting capitalist development in these countries are no longer capable of fulfilling the function of modernising the country. It is not a case of the production relations adjusting themselves to the development of the productive forces. Rather, the productive forces are developed to correspond to the production relations and these are decided upon and organised by political forces. Marx's model is "atoning" for its disregard of this in the serious and often dramatic problems which affect the democratic development of these countries.

As regards his model being a law of motion of history, Marx wrote in the preface to the first edition of *Capital*:

> "And even when a society has got upon the right track for the discovery of the natural laws of its movement — and it is the ultimate aim of this work, to lay bare the economic law of motion of modern society — it can neither clear by bold leaps, nor remove by legal enactments, the obstacles offered by the successive phases of its normal development. But it can shorten and lessen the birth-pangs."

With the advent of new forms of socialist revolution which no longer correspond to Marx's model this observation no longer holds good either. Under certain conditions it *is* possible for societies which have hit upon the right track of their natural law of motion to leap over certain stages of development and abolish them by decree, though it is true that they then have to undertake certain tasks and fulfil certain functions which, in the classic model, were taken care of in the stages which have been leapt over and abolished. The development of society in conformity with certain laws is only brought about, and only modified, by men.

Does this mean, then, that Marx's model must be stood on its head and that socialist revolutions are only possible in backward countries? It is a thesis which finds support in many different quarters. By bourgeois publicists, who say that Marx and Lenin are only relevant to the East (which means that they have shunted the underdeveloped countries of Latin America over to the East). But the idea is supported also by a number of Marxists living in the developed capitalist countries who see no prospect of socialism and have no confidence in the working-class movement of these countries ever playing a revolutionary role — and to whom one might apply the remark made by Marx as a young man that such people are satisfied to be the philosophical contemporaries of the present without becoming its historical contemporaries. And after all (it may be said) are there not already indications in Lenin that the backward countries stand a better chance of revolutionary developments? In a letter of 20th August 1918 he wrote to the American workers saying:

> "We know that circumstances brought our Russian detachment of the socialist proletariat to the fore not because of our merits, but because of the exceptional backwardness of Russia ..."[12]

Leaving aside the point that in this letter Lenin was modestly understating the special services of the revolutionary Russian working-class movement, he was always nevertheless convinced that, sooner or later, the developed capitalist countries, which did not have "Russia's special features", would experience a revolution on the lines of Marx's classic model. And on the other hand the facts tell against any indiscriminate praise of backwardness as such. There are plenty of countries in Asia, Africa and Latin America which are the very reverse of storm centres of world revolution. It is perfectly true that the untapped resources of the anti-feudal and anti-imperialist revolutions have opened up new possibilities for the development of socialist revolutions: in a number of underdeveloped countries in Asia, Africa and Latin America the quantity of revolutionary

[12] *Collected Works*, Vol. 28, p. 75.

factors in the anti-imperialist, nationalist, anti-feudal struggles is exploding into a new quality, a socialist orientation — often the only possible course to take for the conquest of backwardness. But it needs a special combination of objective and subjective factors to transform these possibilities into actualities.

However, we are still left with the basic fact: there are a whole string of countries where the capitalist forces of production had not yet come into conflict with the capitalist relations of production which have abolished capitalist property relations. Equally, there are only two advanced capitalist countries — Czechoslovakia and East Germany — which *have* taken this step. Not a single one of the other advanced capitalist countries has done so. Here we find ourselves up against the basic question of the Marxist conception of history, and the chief problem of the modern working-class movement.

II

MODERN CAPITALISM AND REVOLUTION

Does Marx's model accord with the contradictions and prospects of capitalism as we see it today? Is the fact that hitherto the socialist revolution has taken place almost exclusively in backward countries a sign that it will never take place in countries where capitalism is fully developed? Are the production relations of mature capitalism no longer an obstacle to the expansion of the productive forces, so that the law of motion no longer applies to the very countries for which it was worked out? In the controversy with Bernstein, Rosa Luxemburg always argued that if the development of capitalism no longer involves increasing anarchy then socialism is no longer necessary, and the ultimate goal of the working-class movement disappears.

It has become fashionable when discussing the problems of modern capitalism to point to Bernstein and credit him with having foreseen, and predicted, the real theoretical difficulty presented by modern capitalism, namely, its capacity for finding ways of adapting itself so as to modify and overcome its chief contradiction. However, there is a noteworthy lecture of Bernstein's which indicates that the starting-point of his reflections was the thesis (which he sought to support statistically) that the number of independent producers, capitalists, entrepreneurs and farmers was increasing, and that consequently the chief contradiction of capitalist society was diminishing. The development of modern capitalism demonstrates the exact opposite: the social character of production and the private character of the appropriation of the means of production and of the product stand in ever sharper contrast. On the one hand we get an expansion of the state-owned sector of the economy; measures involving governmental guidance and regulation of the economy, and government investment, are of increasing importance; it becomes increasingly necessary for the state to assume important economic functions in the name of the public interest. On the other hand, the process of concentration is accentuated in both town and countryside: the monopolies take a larger share of production in the shape of direct ownership and control, and agriculture also becomes more concentrated, with the number of independent producers diminishing. The social character of production becomes increasingly apparent, while the private ownership of the means of production and private appropriation of the product are increasingly restricted. In this respect the development of modern capitalism has fully confirmed Marx's model.

Indeed, one may go further: production techniques reach a level where decisive sectors of production become so essential to the life of the community that their development becomes quite impossible on the basis of private ownership of the means of production. In the age of automation, space exploration and atomic energy the capitalist relations of production become superfluous and absurd when it comes to those sectors of production that relate to the future. The powerful role of science also as a productive force, and the collective character of research, bear witness to the increasingly social character of production.

Albert Einstein was already pointing out in his day that there were decisive branches of production where new developments were taking place which were so important for society that they called for control by society; and Norbert Wiener, the pioneer of cybernetics, gave warning of the catastrophic results which would follow automation if "free enterprise" continued to exist. On 22nd March 1964 a number of distinguished scientists, including Myrdal and Pauling, sent the American President a memorandum in which they emphasised that automation makes nonsense of the basis of capitalist society and capitalist distribution. Automation opens up the prospect of boundless, unlimited production for the benefit of mankind, but the existing property relations and market economy "act as a powerful brake on the virtually unlimited potentialities of automated production". Mr. Wilson, as leader of the Labour Party, spoke in a similar vein when addressing the Labour Party conference in 1963 on "Labour and the Scientific Revolution". He said:

> "Since technological progress left to the mechanism of private industry and private property can lead only to high profits for a few, a high rate of employment for a few, and to mass redundancies for the many, if there had never been a case for socialism before, automation would have created it."

Thus scientists and politicians who are far from being Marxists confirm the chief contradiction of Marx's law of motion. The facts speak for themselves. It is certainly no accident that the capitalist society which has developed automation farthest has a considerable pool of permanent unemployment, and the American corporations, wedded as they are to capitalism, will sooner or later come smack up against the problem of the structure of society.

And yet Marx's model does not quite fit: the increasing contradiction between the social character of the productive forces and the private character of the means of production has not resulted in any socialist revolutions, and the countries which are most developed economically — the U.S.A., Britain and West Germany — are the countries where revolutionary socialism is still weak. History has not borne out the idea which revolutionary socialists considered to be confirmed by the great economic crisis of the 1920s and 1930s (and to be supported by various texts from Marx), that the chief contradiction of the law of motion of capitalist society leads to ever deeper economic crises and increasing misery and, as a corollary, to revolutionary convictions among the working masses.

Otto Bauer, in his important work *Zwischen Zwei Weltkriegen* (Between Two World Wars) recalled the point made by Marx and Engels that it was the world economic crisis of 1847 which really gave birth to the February and March revolutions of 1848, and that when industrial prosperity returned, coming to full bloom in 1848—50, that put fresh life into European reaction and gave it new strength. Thinking along the same lines — impressed by the world economic crisis and by the fact that the October Revolution was the consequence of the First World War — Otto Bauer drew the conclusion that new proletarian revolutions would not be likely to succeed except as the result of a Second World War, which would be followed in the capitalist countries by "worse and worse crises, and times of more and more dreadful unemployment and increasing impoverishment for the masses".[1]

After the war, not least as a result of the victorious socialist revolutions, the development of the capitalist countries has in fact taken a very different course.

The Turning Point

Between the two world wars the working-class movement was shaped by the influence of the world economic crisis. Inevitably this appeared to be a triumphant confirmation of the basic contradiction of the law of motion of capitalism. It also strengthened the idea (which cannot be de-

[1] Bratislava, 1963 p. 331.

duced unequivocally from the writings of Marx and Engels) that this basic contradiction is bound up with ever deepening economic crises and an absolute increase in impoverishment. This was felt to be typical, fundamental, and essential to the awakening of revolutionary consciousness and to the creation of a revolutionary situation. Various passages in the *Communist Manifesto* and the *Critique of the Gotha Programme* appeared to support this idea. True, other passages in *Capital*, and in Engels' critique of the Erfurt Programme of the German Social-Democrats, could be set against these ones. But what seemed decisive was the passage in *Capital* formulating the general law of capitalist accumulation, where Marx foresaw the expansion of the productive forces being accompanied by an increase in the industrial reserve army, that is, in the numbers thrown out of work, and in the pauperisation of a section of the working class. Lenin, in his work *The Collapse of the Second International* (June 1915) had written:

"A Marxist cannot have any doubt that a revolution is impossible without a revolutionary situation; furthermore, not every revolutionary situation leads to a revolution. What, generally speaking, are the symptoms of a revolutionary situation? We shall certainly not be mistaken if we point to the following three main symptoms: (1) when it is impossible for the ruling classes to maintain their rule in an unchanged form; when there is a crisis, in one form or another, among the "upper classes", a crisis in the policy of the ruling class which causes fissures, through which the discontent and indignation of the oppressed classes burst forth. Usually, for a revolution to break out it is not enough for the "lower classes to refuse" to live in the old way; it is necessary also that the "upper classes should be unable" to live in the old way; (2) when the want and suffering of the oppressed classes have become more acute than usual; (3) when, as a consequence of the above causes, there is a considerable increase in the activity of the masses, who in "peace time" quietly allow themselves to be robbed, but who in turbulent times are drawn both by the circumstances of the crisis and by the "upper classes" themselves into independent historical action."[2]

In the corresponding definition which Lenin gave in his *Left-Wing Communism* the second point is omitted. Nevertheless, even Kautsky, under the impact of developments between the two world wars, was still capable

[2] Collected Works, Vol. 21 p. 213—14.

of stating expressly that if it were really possible for the standard of living of working people to be substantially improved under capitalism, then the whole business of socialism would have to be abandoned.[3]

Yet already by the turn of the century the standard of living in the most important advanced countries was steadily rising, and though economic crises occurred more or less regularly they were certainly not getting worse each time. The world war and the world economic crisis drove these facts out of the consciousness of the working-class. But the establishment after the Second World War of a system of public ownership, in which capitalist relationships have been and are being superseded, has brought about an entirely new situation in the advanced capitalist countries. Just as feudalism, in competing with the new bourgeois states, developed into "enlightened despotism", so similarly — the comparison originates with the historian Ernst Wangermann[4] — capitalism in its competition with the new social system has developed into a capitalism which pursues, and has to pursue, a policy of managing the economy and regulating investment so as to offset cyclical fluctuations and tendencies towards stagnation. First, it takes account of the fact that production is becoming increasingly social in character; as we noted earlier on, Engels had already remarked on the fact that even the bourgeoisie is capable of recognising the heightened social character of production and including that in its calculations. Second, in pursuance of an economic development uninterrupted by severe or prolonged crises, and on the basis of a continual increase in productivity, various consumer goods, new and old, are brought within the reach of large numbers of working people which in the old days would have seemed quite beyond them. State intervention indicates the strengthening of the social character of production, and thus of one of the component parts of the basic contradiction of the law of motion of capitalism. But at the same time it blunts this contradiction, especially in its political aspect, because it mitigates and modifies the workings of an anarchistic competitive capitalist economy.

This situation of rivalry between the two systems makes it easier for the workers to achieve increases in real wages, to raise their standard of living substantially and to counter the worst distress, where it still occurs, by advances in the social services, etc. The result is that the forms which modern wretchedness takes under modern capitalism — premature aging, and

[3] K. Kautsky: *Die materialistische Geschichtsauffassung* (The Materialist Conception of History) Vol. II p. 563
[4] In an article in *New Left Review* no. 23, Jan.-Feb. 1964.

nervous and vascular diseases, resulting from the hectic pace and increased intensity of work — are felt less acutely in our glittering consumer society than the earlier classic forms of wretchedness were. This is all the truer because in this new situation of rivalry the old forms of sweated labour cannot be practised much more and the exploiting classes have to turn to more refined methods of raising productivity and increasing prices in order to go on getting a return in the new situation. The basic contradiction of capitalist society, an expression of the basic contradiction of the law of motion of history, finds clear enough expression even in modern capitalism: in apparent crises, real crises and recessions — and in a continuous inflation, to which measures of state intervention and public investment within the confines of capitalism are notoriously bound to lead. And, time and again, some searchlight exposes the moral rottenness of capitalist relationships, where now as always, profit counts for more than the common interest — for example in the Contergan scandal, or the dam catastrophe in North Italy, where the Sade Trust continued operations, in spite of many warnings, so as not to lose their invested capital.

However, the forms which this contradiction takes are not in any way bound up with increasing misery, and, so far, certainly not with any automatic growth of revolutionary consciousness among working people. They do not, by themselves, usher in an epoch of social revolution in the developed capitalist countries.

Yet even without deepening economic crises and increasing misery, the forms which the contradiction takes are sufficiently provocative. For profit is still the motive force of production; it is profit that decides which goods are produced, what form they shall take, what people shall want to buy, and what waste is to be organised; the worker — the producer — is not asked what he should produce, and on top of that (as Marx said) his alienation from production is completed by his alienation in consumption:

> "Thus production does not just produce an object for the subject; it also produces a subject for the object ... because it turns the products, which are produced in the first place as objects, into necessary articles of consumption."[5]

It is the contradiction inherent in an economy based on private profit, also, which explains the phenomenon which the American

[5] Marx: *Grundrisse der Kritik der Politischen Ökonomie* (Berlin 1953) p. 53.

economist Professor Galbraith calls "public squalor alongside private affluence":

"The expansion of the private sector supplies what we need least to the detriment of what we need most."[6]

The contradiction within the capitalist profit-making economy leaves us with the social, historical and moral necessity of overthrowing capitalism. But the recognition of necessity, which is necessary to the realisation of that necessity, does not spring, in the advanced capitalist countries, from increasing misery, even though a considerable number of people are still in a state of poverty.

The Despair of C. Wright Mills

This problem has been put most clearly by C. Wright Mills in *The Marxists*.[7] What he stressed all the time was that so far not a single advanced capitalist country has carried through a socialist revolution. (In so saying he overlooked Czechoslovakia.) Marx's model has broken down in the capitalist countries because Marx was familiar only with Victorian capitalism and did not foresee how capitalist property relations would be overthrown in the backward countries, forcing modern capitalism into rivalry. The model breaks down on another count, because it depends upon making a fetish of the working class, upon a "labour metaphysic". But the exploited classes are not necessarily the rising classes: the feudal state was not created by slaves nor was bourgeois society created by serfs. The fact that a class is economically indispensable does not automatically result in that class taking over leadership of the state, and if a class is socially superfluous that does not inevitably lead to its disappearance. In modern capitalist countries the working class is not a revolutionary vanguard; it is a dependent rather than an independent variable, an ingredient of the capitalist system. Since crises are not getting worse and poverty is not increasing, since the sale of commodities more often results in superabundance (obsolescence) than in

[6] *New York Herald Tribune*, 17th January 1964. (C.f. his book *The Affluent Society*, 1958. Trs.)

[7] First published 1962; Pelican ed. 1963. This progressive American sociologist is probably best known for his study of the American ruling class which he called *The Power Elite*. He died in 1962 at the early age of 46. (Trs.)

crises, and since, instead of any growth in class-consciousness, the thoughts and emotions of the masses are moulded by the commercialised means of communication which accentuate political apathy, it follows that there are no grounds for supposing that things will be any different in the foreseeable future or that socialist revolutions will occur in the advanced capitalist countries.

But at the same time Mills acknowledged that there was a prospect of overthrowing the capitalist social structure and emphasised that it was essential not to sit waiting for a crisis but to address oneself to fundamental political reforms and indeed to politically motivated revolutions. But since he did not see the working-class having any historical part to play in this development his avowal sounds hollow, abstract and pessimistic.

Mills was under the spell of conditions in the United States, with its relatively high standard of living, an absence of any strong political movement among the workers and with corruption in the trade union apparatus. Therefore he apparently addressed himself mainly to the liberal intellectuals whom he wished to interest in Marxism. In so doing it seems to me that he underestimated a number of significant trends even within the United States. Thanks to automation even the American working class, increasing numbers of them too, find themselves face to face with the problems of the structure of society. The Negro movement (which Mills ignores in his book) has more than just a democratic element in it; it also includes several proletarian features. The Negroes who constitute only 10 per cent of the population, amount to 20 per cent. of the labour force, and in the automobile industry, mining and lumbering to as much as 30 to 50 per cent. And in any case things are different in Western Europe; this sub-continent has a political working-class movement with a wealth of great traditions and in a number of countries strong revolutionary parties.

All the same, in considering the problems we have been discussing, it would be a mistake to ignore the questions posed by Mills. He is entirely in the right and argues like a Marxist when he insists that the indispensability of the working class does not automatically lead to working-class power, nor the superfluousness of capitalists to the collapse of capitalism. He is entirely in the right and argues like a realist when he insists that the contradiction between the social character of production and the private character of the ownership of the means of production — though still growing under modern capitalism — does not necessarily lead to an epoch of social revolution. It may also lead in the countries in question to an epoch of social decadence, of increasing alienation and spiritual stagnation, giving the superfluous obsolete exploiting classes the chance to set up reactionary terrorist regimes.

Modern Capitalism and the Working-Class Movement

The contradiction between the relations of production and the forces of production takes new forms under modern capitalism. Measures involving intervention and regulation by the state are so widespread that while they certainly do not abolish existing property relations they influence them sufficiently, they modify them sufficiently, to prevent the basic contradiction of capitalist society expressing itself in ever-increasing economic crises and increasing misery. It follows that the law of motion of history will also necessarily assume different forms from those it has assumed hitherto. And therefore the working-class movement must work out a strategy which takes these changes into account. If they do not recognise the changes going on in modern capitalism they will not be able to overthrow it. It is human beings who make the law of motion a real thing.

Capitalism even in its modern form — more especially in its modern form — is senseless, dangerous to life and obsolete; and under modern capitalism especially, the capitalist class shows itself to be unnecessary and superfluous. The working-class movement uses the rivalry between the two systems to secure wage increases and social and political improvements. The movement must also make use of it to exact measures involving intervention and regulation by the state which have a direct effect on property relations, the relations of production, so as to undermine the influence of big business, transferring the ownership of big capital to the state and subjecting it to public control. These measures of public ownership, planning and investment must be combined with other measures to ensure that already now, before they have yet become the decisive force in society, the workers shall have a share in the management of the economy and of individual firms. A many-sided struggle along these lines, involving direct interference in the relations of production, which would correspond to the social character of the productive forces, assist the expansion of the productive forces and take account of the leading role of the producers in society — such a struggle would be able to force big business to retreat and ensure more power and influence over the economy for the working class. It would also safeguard the independence of the working-class movement, freeing it from the all-embracing tentacles of big business and the dope of commercialism and would open up, step by step, the way to the socialist revolution. The sum total of such transitional and intermediate aims, both economic and political in their nature, which would curb the power of the monopolies and give the workers a voice in the running of the state even before the workers assume leadership in the state, and which thanks to their increasing control over the state and the economy would put fresh life and urgency into their demand for the transformation of society — for all this the Italian Communist leader Togliatti coined the phrase "structural reform". Their realisation would solve the contradiction of the law of motion in a new way and would avoid waiting about for those more acute forms of struggle which used to be considered essential for the social revolution.

There are indications of this approach in the classic writers too. For example, in an article on the trade unions of 20th February 1881 Engels wrote:

> "In every struggle of class against class the immediate goal that is being struggled for is political power. The ruling class is defending its political supremacy, that is to say, its safe majority in the legislative bodies. The lower classes fight, in the first place, for a share in this power and subsequently for complete power, in order to arrive at a position where they can alter existing laws to suit their own needs and interests."[8]

Here, in the picture of the stages by which the working class gets a share of political power, there is embodied the idea of stages in the socialist revolution. Similar reflections are to be found in Lenin's writings. Thus at a conference of Party journalists, held on 12th and 13th June 1909, he gave the Bolshevik group in the Duma the job of drawing the masses into political and economic struggle so as to "transform half-hearted and hypocritical reforms under the existing system into strong-points for a working-class movement advancing towards the complete emancipation of the proletariat."[9]

Nonetheless, the emphasis on structural reform in our own day is something fundamentally new. It springs from the fact that the relationship between the forces of production and the relations of production has

[8] Marx—Engels *Werke* Vol. XIX p. 258.
[9] Collected Works Vol. 15 p. 440.

changed to an extent which the classic writers could not foresee, with the result that the contradiction between the forces of production and the relations of production does not have the sort of consequences which can convince the masses of the need for a socialist revolution on the grounds of increasing misery.

The new strategy — and this applies to the backward countries even — must take account of the fact that it is the practical demonstration of the superiority of socialism which really carries conviction. Otto Bauer had already written with regard to the first Soviet Five Year Plan about the vital importance of demonstrating "in practice, the economic, social and cultural superiority of a socialist order of society", and had seen the attraction of socialist ideas as being largely dependent upon "whatever attraction their prototype has for the world's workers".[10] It is upon the demonstration of this superiority — despite having started from a more backward state — that there hangs the decisive proof of the point that the economy will still function without capitalists — and that it will function better indeed, without vital distortions and signs of crisis. But the development of modern capitalism is such that in the long run higher growth rates will not suffice to demonstrate this. In order to achieve a real break-through of socialist ideas in the advanced capitalist countries the new way of life must also offer convincing proof that it guarantees the higher human qualities: a better education, a superior morality, more meaning to life and more democracy.

Since the desire for socialism in the advanced capitalist countries is not going to draw its strength from increasing misery and inhuman living conditions, and since moral, democratic and cultural considerations will play an ever greater part, it will also be necessary to re-assess the role of intellectuals in the working-class movement. Thanks to the part they play in modern techniques of production, in automation and in the management of industry and the economy, they are coming to advocate the very arguments which have taken on significance in winning people for socialist ideas. In so doing they are fulfilling a function reminiscent of the beginning of the modern working-class movement, when they carried the science of socialism to the working masses. Kautsky, in his critique of the Vienna programme of the Austrian social democrats (1909), and Lenin, in *What is to be Done?* (1902), both pointed to the fact that socialist consciousness, scientific socialism, has to be imported into the working-class movement

[10] Op. cit. pp. 211, 221.

from outside, by intellectuals. In the revolutions in Asia, Africa and Latin America the intellectuals are once more fulfilling this historic role, though admittedly under completely different conditions, amongst peoples where the revolutionary movement consists in the main of peasants. In the advanced capitalist countries the problem arises on a new level. Intellectual and moral arguments are becoming increasingly decisive in attracting people to the idea of socialism; and as Marx in particular realised long ago, automation opens up the prospect of a society where the main social problem will be the employment of leisure. The working-class movement's strict formula for the future, "He who does not work, neither shall he eat", will seem as antiquated as it really is. We must develop intellectual and moral arguments which correspond to the changed conditions if the vision of socialism is not to be obliterated from the consciousness of the working class movement. Because, too, only socialism can bridge the gulf between the advanced capitalist countries and the developing countries. When the leading American industrialist L. T. Rader declared "that from a strictly technical point of view it is now possible to produce enough sustenance for all the hungry, to change sea-water into fresh water and to irrigate the deserts", but added that "this is not yet possible economically", he was thinking of the capitalist economy based on private profit, which does mean hunger for the majority of the earth's inhabitants.

In his book *Capitalism, Socialism and Democracy* (1942), in which he concluded gloomily that the role of the entrepreneur was dying out, the economist J. A Schumpeter reproached the intellectuals with organising distrust of capitalism and "actively working for the destruction" of capitalist society. The function of those he criticized is summed up in this criticism.

This approach seems to me essential to helping the law of motion of history to make its break-through in the conditions of modern capitalism. This does not mean that it will necessarily occur in the foreseeable future. It is quite possible to have glittering although stagnating consumer societies and even authoritarian welfare states without its resulting in this break-through to a socialist society. The law of motion of history is an intimation of the necessity of social development taking a certain course; but *when* it takes this course depends on a great many factors, and above all on human beings.

What propaganda for the socialist way forward must clearly emphasize is this: the countries in which the socialist revolution have been victorious so far have been, almost without exception, backward countries, mostly

8*

without democratic traditions. The structures which were erected after the revolution bore the stamp of this backwardness and of this past; and the more backward the country was, the more conspicuous this was. The few industrially advanced countries which constituted the exceptions to this development largely copied the first model, thus damaging the attraction of the socialist idea. In the advanced capitalist countries which have strong democratic and parliamentary traditions the socialist revolution will work out differently; it is bound to work out differently. Above all, it can only come about if large sections of the community are convinced that the revolution, by eliminating private capital, will result in further freedoms being added to the existing democratic freedoms and liberties, and that it will decisively enlarge the scope of democracy.

THE WORLD REVOLUTION

We come round again to our starting point: a philosophy of life for transforming the world.[1] Marx's model, enriched and modified by Lenin's theory of revolution and by the conclusions to be drawn from the anti-imperialist revolutions in the colonial countries, can still be summed up in the idea: socialism follows capitalism just as capitalism followed feudalism. The transition to socialism — and this was just as true of the transition from feudalism to capitalism — does not take place with a fanfare of trumpets, or like the hand-over in a relay race which is being timed by a stop-watch. It is the essential content of an entire period, which can either be called the general crisis of capitalism, if one is emphasising the historical obsolescence of capitalist property relations, or alternatively — if one is emphasising the forces making for change — the period of the world socialist revolution. The rapid development of the productive forces justifies the idea that the socialist revolutions will follow each other in the various different countries more rapidly than the capitalist revolutions did.

All the same, it is still a fairly long period. The transition does not occur spontaneously in the way it did with earlier forms of society. The form it takes, and when it happens, depends above all on how quickly how many people are convinced that the new is also the better — on how many people, convinced that the change is necessary, actually make it necessary by involving themselves in it. The development of the productive forces explains why the intervals between the transition from one social formation to another will get constantly shorter; but even in the age of automation the transition will not be automatic. The law of motion of society includes human activity, and life — as Lenin used to emphasise — is richer and more colourful than theory.

The world revolution began in a backward country and it has been carried forward (almost without exception) in other backward countries where the capitalist relations of production had not become in any way fetters upon the productive forces developing within them. Instead, pre-

[1] *Weltanschauung der Weltveränderung*: c.f. title of first chapter and footnote on it. (Trs)

capitalist and even sometimes pre-feudal relations have been dissolved at lightning speed and consequently the break-through towards a socialist path has involved organising the sort of development of the productive forces which was seen to in the West by capitalism — a task which the bourgeoisie of these other countries could not fulfil.

Is it a law of the world socialist revolution that it shall triumph first in backward countries? Oskar Lange seems to subscribe to this view when he writes in his book *Entwicklungstendenzen der modernen Wirtschaft und Gesellschaft* (Trends in Modern Economy and Society, p. 25):

"As a result of imperialism, capitalism first came to grief in the less developed countries."

Why, exactly, is not explained. It seems to me that Lange's interpretation of the Marxist view of history has been rather strongly influenced by the thinking of Kautsky and of Stalin. Yet it would have been perfectly possible for the 1918 socialist revolution in central Europe to have succeeded; its defeat was in no way foreordained, although it is true that the defeat had important consequences which did in part have the character of according with natural laws. The fact that the first breach made by the socialist revolution remained an isolated one very largely determined the course of the revolution and its problems, including to some extent the cardinal fact that hitherto the transition to a socialist revolution has taken place almost entirely in backward countries, while the advanced capitalist countries have remained capitalist: being ripe for revolution on the material plane does not necessarily result in a subjective readiness for revolution.

Recently this fact has led to the search for a theoretical generalisation about it by the Chinese Communists and by those Marxists in Western countries who are in sympathy with their ideas. The storm centres of the world revolution (they say) are Asia, Africa and Latin America; in these continents the reserves of the agrarian and national revolutions make it easier to achieve the break-through to the socialist revolution. The comparison drawn by the Indonesian Communists is very significant: just as the revolution in China won its first victories in the villages and then went on, from the villages, to capture the towns, so the socialist revolution will first be victorious in the underdeveloped countries and will then go on, from there, to conquer the developed industrial nations. How?

At the beginning of September 1965 the leading Communist Lin Piao made a speech in Peking on the twentieth anniversary of the defeat of Japan which amongst other things contained this passage:

"The peasantry are the leading force in the national democratic revolutions . . . Only the countryside can offer wide expanses in which the revolutionaries can manoeuvre freely. Taking the whole globe, one may consider North America and West Europe as 'the world's towns' and Asia, Africa and Latin America as 'the world's villages' . . . In a certain sense the world revolution at the present day consists in the encirclement of the town by the country districts."

Here the tactics of partisan warfare adopted by the Chinese Communists are extended to the whole world, thus blandly ignoring the fact that reaction reigns in many of the 'villages'. And in the world of the atom bomb I am reluctant to carry this over-simplified military comparison to its logical conclusion. The tragedy of the Indonesian Communists demonstrates the fallaciousness of an un-Marxist concept which abandons any real Marxist analysis of the 'village'.

Some American Marxists have declared the 'sated' workers of the advanced nations to be incapable of any revolutionary activity, and have pinned their hopes on a flood of anti-colonial revolutions. But who is going to relieve the workers in the capitalist countries of the task of altering their countries' structure? Here, modification of Marx's model in accordance with the facts has led to a sectarian world outlook of just enduring the world and to the passive renunciation of the transformation of the very world for which Marx's model was designed.

On the other hand it cannot be denied that if in the course of social development "a few revolutions" do come along this releases an astonishing amount of energy for several more revolutions to develop. Marx remarked about the bourgeois revolutions of 1848 that they were "little cracks and rifts in the hard crust of European society. They disclosed the abyss. Under the apparently solid surface they revealed oceans of liquid matter which only needed expanding to make the continent of solid rock shatter into fragments."[2]

In one sense the revolutions in Asia, Africa and Latin America confirm this picture. But can the socialists in the countries where the modern working-class movement had its birth be satisfied with applauding the world revolution from the dress-circle of the 'welfare state'?

[2] Speech at the anniversary celebrations of the *People's Paper*, 14th April 1856. (Reprinted in *Marx and Engels on Britain*, 1954.)

Parallels

Drawing parallels with the way earlier forms of society superseded one another proves nothing, but it is suggestive. It shows at any rate that, before reality modified Marx's model, his model did (as a model should) extract the essentials — the structure, the framework. In any given country the transition often involved hybrid forms, with old and new relations of production side by side (and Marx and Engels pointed these out, too). Sometimes the transition was largely brought about by external influences. In Eastern Europe and Asia the advance of capitalism occurred partly in connection with the economic penetration of the country by imperialism. The objective need for one society to be superseded by another has not by any means always resulted in a rapid change taking place. Regimes based on slavery have disintegrated thanks to inner corruption and outside attack and become stagnant and decadent without this resulting in a transition to feudalism. The need to abolish serfdom was felt, and even voiced, for a long time before the revolution abolishing it actually occurred. Forms of society which are doomed to destruction, which are obsolete and outdated, can go on for a long time passing through painful periods of corruption and decadence without disappearing. Objective readiness for supersession does not as a matter of course result in subjective readiness for it, certainly not in the past when the subjective forces were not always clear about what to substitute for the system which was in decay.

It is well known that the supersession of feudal relations of production has not always taken the form of the incompatibility between the forces of production and the relations of production coming dramatically to a head. In certain decisive countries a considerable industrial expansion occurred well before the political revolution, and the bourgeois revolution took place at a period when bourgeois relations of production were already in being, though they were admittedly hindered and hampered by the institutions of feudalism.

It has been a basic tenet among Marxists that things will be different in the case of the socialist revolution and that only the seizure of power by the proletariat will make possible the socialisation of the means of production. But nowadays this problem, too, is more complicated than that. The social character of production is forcing its way through even on capitalist soil and within a capitalist integument; and in the advanced capitalist countries the working-class movement is confronted with the task of achieving, stage by stage, structural reforms which will confine and reduce the positions of power held by big business, and of forcing through, even before the proletariat has achieved the political leadership of society, the sort of measures which one used to envisage as being possible only if they had, indeed, already captured the leadership of the state. It is not simply a matter of reforms, but of *structural* reforms, which can only be brought about through tremendous struggles and conflicts.

The most fascinating, important and accurate thing in Marx's model is its broad direction. The development of the productive forces obviously necessitates measures to control the anarchy of an economy based on competition and profit, and forms of regulation and planning; even the capitalist states are driven to this nowadays. Thus in their own way they confirm Marx's law of motion even before the workers of these countries have become one of the decisive, and ultimately the decisive, force which carries through the measures which are logically necessary to the development of the productive forces and which lead towards the abolition of capitalist property relations.

Marx and Engels assumed that the victory of the working class would occur first in the advanced capitalist countries; and moreover that it would occur simultaneously. The first part of the prophecy has been refuted by history. The second part may be confirmed to a large extent, in the form of one broad gradual development within the different countries of Western Europe.

Peaceful and Violent Revolution

The essential content of the socialist revolution consists in the transformation of the relations of production, whether this happens in a peaceful or violent way. Writing in the 1840s and 1850s Marx' and Engels' ideas about the socialist revolution were still determined by the pattern of the French Revolution and by the course of the 1848 revolution, and the struggles on the barricades. At that date Marx and Engels insisted that capitalism would have to be overthrown forcibly, by civil war; that force is the midwife of every society pregnant with a new one *(Contribution to a Critique of the Hegelian Philosophy of Law)*; that in the last resort the struggles of class against class amount to the brutal clash of man against man *(The Poverty of Philosophy)*. The *Communist Manifesto*, too, declares that the class struggle, the more or less veiled civil war, reaches a point where it breaks out into open revolution and where the violent overthrow of the bourgeoisie lays the foundation for the sway of the proletariat. The concluding part of the *Communist Manifesto* contains the famous avowal of the Communists:

"They openly declare that their ends can be attained only by the forcible overthrow of all existing social conditions."

In the 1860s and 1870s their ideas became more subtle and it was more often pointed out that different paths are possible, that these depend on the conditions in individual countries. Only one must have no illusions about the exploiting classes, for these will always, whatever the circumstances, do everything they can to prevent the victory of the working class. Thus Marx and Engels agreed that in England it looked as if it might be possible to "buy out the whole gang" — without, however, having any illusions about the gang. In 1886, in the preface to the English edition of *Capital*, Engels wrote that Marx's study of the economic history and condition of England led him the conclusion that "at least in Europe, England is the only country where the inevitable social revolution might be effected entirely by peaceful and legal means. He certainly never forgot to add that he hardly expected the English ruling classes to submit without a 'pro-slavery rebellion' to this peaceful and legal revolution."

And Marx and Engels envisaged the possibility of a peaceful revolution not only in England but apparently in America too, where at that date there was also no developed military-bureaucratic state machine. That is the significance of Marx's comment in his letter to his friend Kugelmann (12th April 1871) that "on the continent" the smashing of the machinery of the state is the essential preliminary to every real peoples' revolution. Marx formulated his position more precisely in an interview with *The World* on 3rd July 1871 — that is, a short while after the events of the Paris Commune:

"In every part of the world different aspects of the problem emerge. The workers take these into account and approach the solution in their own particular way. The organisations of the workers cannot be absolutely identical, down to the last detail, in Newcastle and Barcelona, in London and Berlin. In England, for example, the way is open to the working class to develop their political power how they will. There an uprising would be foolishness, when the goal can be reached more quickly and certainly through peaceful agitation. In France the great number of repressive laws and the deadly antagonism between the classes seems to necessitate a violent solution of the social conflicts.

Whether such a solution is actually adopted is a matter for the working class of that country. The International does not take it upon itself to dictate on this question, and scarcely even to offer advice."[3]

This accords with the reference to the possibility of the two alternatives made at the London congress of the International on 21st September 1871:

"We must explain to the governments: We know that you are the armed might directed against the proletariat; we shall proceed against you in a peaceful way where that is possible for us, and with weapons if it should become necessary."[4]

As a further illustration it is worth noting a speech made by Marx at a meeting in Amsterdam on 15th September 1872, after the Hague congress of the International:

"One day the working man must seize political power so as to construct the new organisation of labour; he must overthrow the old political system which supports the old institutions if he does not want, like the early Christians who despised and neglected these things, to forfeit his kingdom of heaven upon earth.

But we have not asserted that the ways of attaining this goal are the same everywhere.

We appreciate that one must take into consideration the institutions and customs and traditions of the different countries, and we do not deny that there are countries like America and England — and were I better acquainted with your institutions I might perhaps add Holland too — where the workers can reach their goals by peaceful means. While that may be true we also have to recognize that in most continental countries the lever of our revolutions has to be force; it is force to which one must some day resort so as to establish the sovereignty of labour."[5]

In this connection it is interesting that Engels, in his criticism of the Erfurt Programme (1891), remarked that in a number of advanced parliamentary countries such as England *and* France (in contrast to Germany) one could conceive of the old society being peacefully superseded by the

[3] Marx—Engels *Werke* Vol. XVII p. 641 (not available in English).
[4] *Ibid* p. 652.
[5] *Ibid*. Vol. XVIII p. 160.

new. Engels was undoubtedly influenced by the relatively peaceful development of the 1880s and 1890s, when the working-class movement was broadening out and the social-democratic parties were scoring great electoral successes. In advising the parties Engels saw it as one of his main tasks, in opposition to anarchists and sectarians, to adapt the tactics of the working-class movement to this "splendid and secure development, which is advancing with the calm and inevitability of a process of nature."[6] The point was, without abandoning the use of revolutionary force in principle, or entertaining illusions about the exploiting classes and the class character of bourgeois democracy, to *make use of* legality and the possibilities offered by democracy.

Engels' attitude on this was also expressed by his according increasing significance to the franchise. In *The Origin of the Family* (1888) it was only the gauge of the maturity of the working-class; in his foreword to *The Condition of the Working-Class in England* (1892) it was an achievement which ought to be used in the interest of the working-class; in 1894, in a letter to the Vienna congress of the Austrian social-democrats he compares it to a weapon which in the hands of a class-conscious proletariat fires further and more accurately than a small bore machine-gun in the hands of a well-drilled soldiery. And in his introduction to Marx's *Class Struggles in France* (1895) he said that universal suffrage, which hitherto had been a means of deception, had become an instrument for the emancipation of the masses; consequently he stressed the importance of campaigning in elections and of utilising the tribunal of parliament.

Engels never entertained any illusions about the exploiting classes' readiness for peace and never preached the renunciation of the use of revolutionary force. He taught the working-class to utilise the relatively peaceful development of those years and, as he wrote in 1892, not to start the shooting.

In the same famous introduction to *Class Struggles in France* (which the Executive Committee of the German Social-Democratic Party would only publish in a censored, garbled version) Engels explicitly emphasised that the proletariat was not renouncing revolution, that the right to revolution was the only real "historical right". However, the 'barricade tactics' of earlier revolutions, which were carried through under the leadership of small bands of determined men, were outdated; it was necessary to adapt oneself to the new military and historical conditions and, above all, to

[6] Letter to Bebel of 24th October 1891.

recognise that the transformation of society requires the support of broad masses of people who have understood what it is all about.

Lenin started off with the thesis that in the imperialist period, thanks to the general development of the power of the executive, "the liberation of the oppressed classes . . . is impossible without violent revolution" *(State and Revolution)*, that the proletarian revolution is unthinkable without civil war *(The Immediate Tasks of the Soviet Government)*, without the "forcible overthrow of the bourgeoisie". (Theses presented to the Second Congress of the Communist International). In a polemic with Otto Bauer (February 1920) Lenin only conceded the possibility of the exploiting classes in some country voluntarily abdicating their sovereignty if the working class had already been victorious in the neighbouring countries and great powers. It was only in special circumstances like that — circumstances which, with the establishment of a group of socialist states, are of course no longer so special as before — that Lenin envisaged the possibility of a peaceful path to socialism, base on "an absolutely secure victory of the proletariat, the absolute hopeledsness of the position of the capitalists, the absolute necessity for them tosdisplay the most scrupulous obedience and their readiness to do so."[7]

It is interesting, then, that even in 1917 Lenin contemplated the possibility of a peaceful path to socialism, that is to say, of the Russian working class being victorious without a civil war. After the February revolution, in his April Theses, he had charged the Bolsheviks with the task of winning a majority in the Soviets and so using the precious opportunity of leading the workers to power peacefully without civil war. He expressly defended the April Theses against the accusation that they tended towards civil war. They directed the party towards "a peaceful period of revolution", towards "a peaceful development" of the revolution *(On Slogans)*. No class was able then (February—July 1917) to resist the decisions of the majority in the Soviets. "This course would have been the least painful, and it was therefore necessary to fight for it most energetically."[8]

After the government had suppressed the July demonstration, Stalin declared at the Sixth Party Congress that the revolution's peaceful period had come to an end. But when the Kornilov revolt of August 1917 saw a shift towards the left in the ranks of the Mensheviks and Socialist-Revolutionaries, Lenin came back once more to the possibility of a "gradual,

[7] Collected Works Vol. 30 p. 361 *(Notes of a Publicist)*.
[8] Collected Works Vol. 25 p. 185

peaceful, gentle" development towards socialism *(A Central Problem of the Revolution)*. Lenin offered to re-establish the alliance with the Socialist-Revolutionaries and Mensheviks, against the Cadets and bourgeoisie, which had proved so valuable in putting down the Kornilov revolt.

"Only an alliance of the Bolsheviks with the Socialist-Revolutionaries and Mensheviks, only an immediate transfer of all power to the Soviets would make civil war in Russia impossible, for a civil war begun by the bourgeoisie against such an alliance, against the Soviets of Workers', Soldiers' and Peasants' Deputies is inconceivable." "The peaceful development of any revolution is, generally speaking, extremely rare and difficult." But "at such an exceptional moment in history, a peaceful development of the revolution is possible, and probable, if all power is transferred to the Soviets." The struggle of parties within the Soviets would then proceed peacefully. "We Bolsheviks will do everything to secure this peaceful development of the revolution." However, Lenin concluded, if the Mensheviks and Socialist-Revolutionaries refuse the offer of an alliance and continue their policy of capitulation to reaction, then civil war will be inevitable.[9]

In his important work *The Tasks of the Revolution* (26—27th September old style; 9—10th October in our calendar) the last chapter is headed "The Peaceful Development of the Revolution". There Lenin talks about its being "the last chance to ensure the peaceful development of the revolution". If the Soviets take power into their hands nine-tenths of the population would welcome it and the exploiting classes would not be able to offer any resistance:

> "A possibility very seldom to be met with in the history of revolutions now faces the democracy of Russia, the Soviets and the Socialist-Revolutionary and Menshevik parties, ... to ensure the peaceful development of the revolution, peaceful election of deputies by the people, and a peaceful struggle of parties inside the Soviets; they could test the programmes of the various parties in practice and power could pass peacefully from one party to another."

If this opportunity is missed, Lenin concluded, civil war will be inevitable. Victory is absolutely certain, but it would then have to be at the cost of heavy sacrifices. That was why it was so important to seize this last chance for the revolution to develop peacefully.[10]

[9] Collected Works Vol. 26 pp. 36, 37, 42. *(The Russian Revolution and Civil War)*.
[10] Collected Works, Vol. 26 pp. 67—68.

The policy of a peaceful path towards socialism certainly did not imply advancing without any struggles. It was a policy of having things develop without a civil war — *in the least painful way*, as Lenin often said — and, along with that, it expressly envisaged the existence of several parties within the system of working-class power. It was because the Mensheviks and Socialist-Revolutionaries sided with the counter-revolution and foreign intervention that they were stamped out along with it (as Otto Bauer emphasised).

The present division of opinion in the Communist movement has revived the old argument about whether it is ever possible for a socialist revolution to proceed peacefully. A lot of those who say it is possible point to the establishment of a number of people's democracies, both in Europe and Asia, where the transformation of the relations of production was not preceded by any civil war. Those who argue against the possibility of peaceful advance retort that in those countries the tasks of the civil war, and above all the whole business of smashing the old machinery of state, were in fact solved by the war and by the military assistance of the Soviet Army. Obviously we cannot settle the question in all these cases simply by labelling them peaceful or unpeaceful (civil war).

As regards those nationalist, anti-imperialist revolutions that have a socialist orientation it is clear that in some countries, such as Vietnam and Algeria, say, the foundations were laid by great armed struggles, while in other countries, like Guinea, Ghana and Mali, the development has been along more or less peaceful lines.

As regards the advanced countries, it is quite true that, putting aside the special case of Czechoslovakia, there has been no instance so far of a peaceful socialist revolution. But there has also been no instance of the working-class winning victory after a civil war, of the socialist revolution triumphing by violence. The idea of a head-on armed clash goes against the instincts of the very forces which would have to see it through — though that does not amount to there being a law that it can be unconditionally avoided. In any case here the problem of the state, of nationalisation and so forth, is much more complicated than in the backward countries and therefore I propose to return to it on another occasion. It is sufficient here to sum up by saying that there is such a great variety of ways towards the socialist revolution, of which the essence is the socialisation of the means of production, that it cannot be confined, either in the advanced or in the underdeveloped countries, to the forms which these revolutions have taken up to now.

As I have said earlier, the decisive content of the world revolution is the socialisation of the means of production — of those means of production, I would add, which are decisive in determining the character of the relations of production. On 14th April 1921, after Georgia had acceded to the Soviet Union, Lenin wrote a letter to the Communists in the Transcaucasian Soviet republics calling upon them "to be fully alive to their special position and that of their republics, as distinct from the position and conditions of the Russian Soviet Republic; to appreciate the need to refrain from copying our tactics, and thoughtfully to vary them according to the different concrete conditions." Lenin went on in this letter to point out that, in contrast to the position in October 1917, there was no immediate danger of imperialist intervention, and that there were great opportunities for organising trade with the West. One could have a more liberal approach to the peasantry and the petty-bourgeois sections, and "make a slower, more cautious and more systematic transition to socialism". "More moderation and caution, and a greater readiness to make concessions to the petty-bourgeoisie, the intelligentsia and especially the peasantry." In October they had to make the first breach in the imperialist system. Now that this breach had been made one should not simply "copy Russian tactics but make an independent analysis of the reasons for their peculiar features, the conditions that gave rise to them and their results. Go beyond the letter and apply the spirit, the essence and the lessons of the experiences of the years 1917—1921."[11]

Later on, this advice from Lenin — like a lot else — was forgotten, and in a whole number of states small businesses were, following the Soviet pattern, abolished and transformed into state and co-operative enterprises, with all the familiar political and economic consequences. It is impossible to predict which of the many diverse forms of economic co-operation will be assumed by handicrafts, agriculture and small businesses in different countries, or whether they may not continue to exist for a long time in their old state even in countries which, on the basis of the socialisation of the decisive means of production, are already being drawn into the process of world revolution.

Socialisation of the means of production does not by itself amount to socialism, but it is the essential thing in the socialist revolution. In the

[11] Collected Works. Vol 32 pp. 316—318.

advanced capitalist countries too, the decisive means of production have to be taken out of the hands of big capital. Nationalisation measures in these countries can be transformed into significant steps on the road to socialism provided they are bound up with moves towards the complete disarming of capital, and provided they give the working people a real say in making decisions about the nationalised undertakings.

Towards New Shores

In *The German Ideology* (1846) Marx spoke of the contradiction between the forces of production and the relations of production resulting in the juxtaposition of contradictions within human consciousness, of its resulting in contradictory forms of consciousness. Louis Aragon, in his novel *Holy Week*, has shown how the transition to new social relations at the beginning of the last century found its expression among the different types and sections of society in the most contradictory ideas and plans and judgments. And are we not experiencing the same sort of thing to-day when we have the profession of Islam and Buddhism being wedded to Marxist concepts?

In the advanced capitalist countries, too, the X-ray of our age enables us to detect the socialist structure. Its avowals and concepts and forms of expression are many and various. Teilhard de Chardin wrote that "Something is happening to the general structure of human consciousness. Another kind of life is beginning." *(Sauvons l'humanité)*. So the papal encyclical *Mater et Magistra* acknowledges the importance of the state in the economic sphere; even modern capitalism has taken up the notion of "planning"; and the great bourgeois economist Schumpeter in his last great work decided, sorrowfully but quite definitely, that the private business man performs no useful function. But these are only minor examples in comparison with the evolutionary theory of the French Jesuit Teilhard de Chardin. In a unique synthesis of theological and scientific elements he concludes by appealing to Christians to be "supporters of development" and to carve a way forward to enable this development to reach its fulfilment — which the Jesuit father calls not socialism but 'Omega'.

"It will be a world where large telescopes and atom-smashers will cost more money and arouse more spontaneous enthusiasm than all the bombs and guns; a world where it will be possible, not merely for organised, subsidised groups of specialists but for the ordinary man in the street to tackle the day-to-day problem of making discoveries about the organisation of matter, about fundamental particles, about the stars. It will be a world — indeed, it is already happening — in which people live, not in order to get, but in order to understand and to be."[12]

This distinction between the world of being and the world of getting was part of the fundamental thinking of the young Marx. The different and contradictory forms of consciousness, born of the same development, jostle and overlap with each other, but point in the same direction. One society is foundering and a new one is rising victorious — provided that humanity safeguards its existence: it is trite but true that mankind cannot develop without human beings and that the law of motion of society does not guarantee it against destruction.

Individuals and classes are making this law a reality, and sooner or later it will be a reality in all countries, as soon as the new society has shown itself to be manifestly better and wiser. When it is showing this in the most varied forms and ways, coupled with the most diverse ideas, then the example of those countries which have already carried through the revolution will play a decisive part.

But the socialisation of the means of production is only the most fundamental thing about the socialist revolution, its foundation; it does not exhaust it. The revolution also involves the distribution and management of the products, and it includes the prospect of ending the alienation of men from production, both in relation to the product and in relation to the organisation and management of production. This is not achieved automatically by the socialisation of the means of production. But without this perspective, without concrete proof that this perspective is realisable under socialism, the struggle for socialism in the advanced capitalist countries will scarcely make much headway. The conviction that the new is also better is the pre-requisite for the realisation of the law of motion of society.

The socialisation of the means of production is the greatest revolution in the history of mankind. It is indissolubly bound up with the elimination

[12] Teilhard de Chardin: 1881—1955. Spent most of his working life in China where he made a special study of prehistoric man. He devoted himself to reconciling religion and modern science, championing especially an evolutionary view of human society as developing gradually towards the Kingdom of God. The church authorities suppressed publication of his books during his lifetime. In the last decade his works (widely translated) have won support amongst both Christians and humanists. (Trs.)

of the power of capital which debases, corrupts, oppresses and destroys. It involves a tremendous revolution in education, and the more backward the country is the more extensive this has to be. The revolution offers the working people real security such as even modern capitalism cannot guarantee; it eliminates the forces interested in profitable wars. What a tremendous advance! Yet even that does not convey all that we mean when we talk about socialism. The socialisation of the means of production creates the preconditions which enable us to come closer to that state of affairs which is what we really and chiefly think of when we speak of socialism, namely, the fullest and freest flowering of the human personality in face of all the power of administration and technique, and the greatest possible participation in political and economic affairs, from the greatest questions down to the smallest details. Man must escape from the danger of being nothing more than a cog in a machine. These socialist hopes are not automatically fulfilled when the means of production are socialised. They can only be brought about on that basis, but they have to be fought for. And the conviction that the socialisation of the means of production is the most important preliminary step in fighting for them must become the conviction of the greatest possible number of people, so that through men the law of motion may be realised and socialism come true as the highest form of humanism.

REFERENCES

Works by Marx, Engels and Lenin discussed or quoted in this book with page references. Arranged in chronological order.

MARX

		page
1844	Contribution to the Critique of Hegel's Philosophy of Law	31n, 121
1845	The Holy Family (with Engels)	22, 40, 48—50
	Theses on Feuerbach	36—7, 37n, 50, 55
1846	The German Ideology (with Engels)	129
1847	The Poverty of Philosophy	121
1848	The Communist Manifesto (with Engels)	18—19, 22, 59, 67, 68, 107, 121—2
1849	Wage-Labour and Capital	59
1850	Address of the Central Committee to the Communist League (with Engels)	68—9
	Class Struggles in France (introd. by Engels, 1895.)	124—5
1852	Eighteenth Brumaire of Louis Bonaparte	52, 52n
1857	Grundrisse der Politischen Ökonomie	38, 53
	including Pre-Capitalist Economic Formations	38n, 87
1859	Critique of Political Economy	16, 55n, 100
1867	Capital, Vol. I	17, 20n, 21—22, 23, 40, 41, 43, 101
1870	Address of the General Council of the First International	65—6
1871	The Civil War in France	23—4
1875	Critique of the Gotha Programme	62, 107
1894	Capital, Vol. III (edited by Engels)	41, 60—1

ENGELS

1847	The Principles of Communism	72—3
1850	The Peasant War in Germany	43
1875	Social Relations in Russia	67—8
1878	Anti-Dühring	19
1883	Socialism: Utopian and Scientific	19—21, 22—3, 62—4
1888	Ludwig Feuerbach	18, 25, 37n
1892	The Condition of the Working Class in England in 1844	22, 124

LENIN

INDEX

Adler, Max, 27
Advanced countries; general failure to develop socialist revolutions, 77, 83 (Lenin), 102—3, 106—9, 118—9; their way forward to socialism, 112—16, 120—1, 121—5 (Marx and Engels)
Algeria, 94—5, 96—9
Aragon, Louis, 129
Automation, 105, 115

Bacon, Sir Francis, 11
Basle Manifesto (1912), 71
Bauer, Otto, 81, 81n, 106, 114, 125
Bernstein, Edward, 26n, 26—7, 104
Bourgeois revolution: as prelude to socialist revolution, 67—72, 77, 79—80, 90—1
Brecht, Bertolt, 45
Bukharin, N. I., 33, 33n, 37, 82
Burchett, Wilfred, 99

Calvez, S. Y., 49
Capitalism, contradictions of, 18—24, 40—1, 59—63, 100—1, 104—6, 108—10, 111—12; (see also Crises, economic)
Chardin, Teilhard de, 129—30, 130n
China and the Chinese revolution, 86, 89—94, 118—9
Class struggle, 32, 40—1, 113, 121—5
Colonial and backward countries, revolution in, 84—103, 118—9; (see also Algeria, China, Cuba, Russia, Vietnam)
Crises, economic: 18ff, 59—60, 106—7; their solution in socialism, 21—8, 62—4; (See also Depression)
Cuba, 94, 96

Dahrendorf, Rolf, 43
Democracy under socialism, 112—16, 131 (See also Bourgeois revolution and Socialist revolution)
Depression, "the great" (1873—96), 20n; of 1929, 59—60, 106
Descartes, René, 11—12, 17
Determinism, 26, 27, 35—7, 51—3, 55—8
Diderot, Denis, 56—7

Eddington, Sir A. S., 47
Einstein, Albert, 105
Engels (See also Marx): his idea of history, 19—23, 30, 38—40, 52; on class struggle and revolution, 67—8 (Russia), 72—3, 113, 121—5 (Western Europe); on monop-

99—100, 102; violent and peaceful revolution, 125—7; wrong for other countries to copy Russia, 128 (See also separate list of works quoted and referred to)
Liebknecht, Karl, 28n
Luxemburg, Rosa, 27—9, 28n, 81, 104

Mao Tse-tung, development of his theory of revolution, 90—4
Marx, his conception of history, 15—24, 31, 38, 40—2, 48—50, 55n, 65, 100, 101, 109, 129; his law of motion of capitalism, 18—24, 40—1, 59, 63, 100—1; on class struggle, 40—1, 48—9; on the prospects of a socialist revolution, 65—6, 68—9, 121—3 (See also separate list of works quoted and referred to); letters to Annenkov (1846), 40; Bolte (1871), 40—1; Engels (1856), 67; Kugelmann (1871), 42, 122; Ruge, 13; speeches at: anniversary of the *Peoples' Paper* (1856), 119; London Congress of First International (1871), 123; Hague Congress of First International (1872), 123; interview with *The World* (1871), 122—3
Mater et Magistra, 129
Mehring, Franz, 57
Mills, C. Wright, 110—12
Mode of production, successive forms of, 16, 87, 100—2, 117, 120—1
Monopoly, development of, 20, 23, 61—5, 73, 104; denied by Bernstein, 26, 104
Myrdal, G., 105

Narodniks, 51n
Nationalisation, 21, 25—6, 64—5, 112—13, 128—9, 130—1 (See also State owner-ship under capitalism)
National Liberation struggles, 84—103; Algeria, 96—9; China, 91—4; Latin America, 96; Lenin on, 84—6, 87—9, 99
Necessity in history, 12—17, 21—2, 26—45, 48, 50, 53—8, 115.

Pacem in Terris, 17
Paris Commune (1871) 23—4, 122
Pauling, Linus, 105
Peasantry, as allies of proletariat in struggle for socialism, 67—70, 74—6, 85; as the leading revolutionary force — in China, 90—4, — in Algeria, Latin America, Vietnam, 95—9
Planck, Max. 46, 57—8
Plekhanov, G. V., 29n, 29—30, 31, 51
Production, control of under socialism, 21, 53, 64
Productive forces; and relations of production, 15—16, 18—21, 59—61, 100; their increasingly social character under capitalism, 18, 20, 61, 64, 104—5 (See also Nationalisation, State ownership)
Proletariat: as gravediggers of capitalism, 22—4, 26, 40—1, 48—9; as leaders of socialist revolution, 67—73, 78—9; this idea modified, 90ff.

Rader, L. T. 115
Reformism, 26n
Relations of production, see Productive forces
Revisionism, 26n

Revisionist controversy, 26—9
Revolution: its aim, 40—1 (Marx), 113 (Engels); when it occurs, 16, 100 (Marx), 107 (Lenin); see also Socialist Revolution
Revolutions of 1848, 59, 119, 121—2
Russia and the Russian revolution: 69—83, 102; constituting the beginning of the world revolution, 85—6, 93—4, 99—100; prospects as seen by Marx and Engels, 67—8

Sartre, J. P., 53—6, 58
Schaff, Adam, 55
Schopenhauer, A., 57
Schroedinger, Erwin, 47
Schumpeter, J. A., 115, 129
Social-Democratic Party, 25n; of Austria, 23; of Germany, 26
Socialism: basis in development of capitalism, 18—28, 40, 48—9, 59—66, 104—6, 120—1; different roads to socialism in different countries, 122—4 (Marx and Engels), 127, 128 (Lenin)
Socialism in one country, 73—4, 81—3
Socialist revolution: as envisaged by Marx and Engels, 22—4, 48—9, 59, 65—6, 67—9, 72—3, 121—5; its inevitability, 18, 22—8, 30, 42—5, 86; Lenin's understanding of its possibility in Russia, 69—75, 78—80; need to achieve it in advanced countries, 112—16; occurring hitherto chiefly in backward countries, 100—3, 117—19; what it means, 128—31 (See also Bourgeois revolution, Violent and peaceful revolution)
Soviet historical interpretation in Stalinist period, 51—3
Spinoza, B. de, 12, 12n
Stalin, J.V., 31, 34, 53, 76, 82—3, 87—8, 125
Standard of living, 108—10
State ownership under capitalism, 63—5, 104, 108 (See also Nationalisation)

Technology, effect of advances in, 18—19, 105
Togliatti, Palmiro, 113
Trotsky, Leon, and permanent revolution, 81—2; and China, 89—90

Vico, Giovanni Batista, 12, 12n
Vietnam and the Vietcong, 89, 99
Violent or peaceful revolution, 121—8 (See also Lenin, theory of revolution)

Wahl, Jean, 42—3
Wangermann, Ernst, 108
Weltanschauung, 11n, 117n
Wiener, Norbert, 105
Wieser, Wolfgang, 47—8
Wilson, Harold, 105
World war and revolution (1914—18), 71, 73, 75—6, 79, 83; (1939—45), 87—9, 106, 108, 110—12

Zinoviev, G., 77